PROCLAMATION COMMENTARIES

- The Old Testament Witnesses for Preaching

Foster R. McCurley, *Editor*

The Eighth Century Prophets

AMOS · HOSEA · ISAIAH · MICAH

Bernhard W. Anderson

FORTRESS PRESS   Philadelphia, Pennsylvania

COPYRIGHT © 1978 BY FORTRESS PRESS

Library of Congress Cataloging in Publication Data

Anderson, Bernhard W
  The eighth century prophets.

  Bibliography: p.
  Includes indexes.
  1. Bible. O.T. Isaiah I–XXXIX–Criticism,
interpretation, etc. 2. Bible. O.T. Minor
prophets–Criticism, interpretation, etc.
I. Title.
BS1515.2.A52   224   78-54545
ISBN 0-8006-0595-0

7115D78 Printed in the United States of America 1-595

THE EIGHTH CENTURY PROPHETS

CONTENTS

EDITOR'S FOREWORD

This present volume continues *Proclamation Commentaries–The Old Testament Witnesses for Preaching*. Like its New Testament counterpart, this series is not intended to replace traditional commentaries which analyze books of the Bible pericope by pericope or verse by verse. This six-volume series attempts to provide background material on selected Old Testament books which, among other things, will assist the reader in using *Proclamation: Aids for Interpreting the Lessons of the Church Year*. Material offered in these volumes consists of theological themes from various witnesses or theologians out of Israel's believing community. It is our expectation that this approach—examining characteristic themes and motifs—will enable the modern interpreter to comprehend more clearly and fully a particular pericope which contains or alludes to such a subject. In order to give appropriate emphasis to such issues in the brief form of these volumes, the authors present the results, rather than the detailed arguments, of contemporary scholarship.

On the basis of its concern to address the specific task of preaching and teaching the Word of God to audiences today, this commentary series stresses the theological dilemmas which Old Testament Israel faced and to which her witnesses responded. Accordingly, the historical and political details of Israel's life and that of her ancient Near Eastern neighbors are left to other books. Selected for discussion here are those incidents and issues in Israel's history which have a direct relationship to the theological problems and responses in her existence. Since the Word of God is always addressed to specific and concrete situations in the life of people, the motifs and themes in these commentaries are directed to those selected situations which best exemplify a certain witness's theology.

The eighth-century prophets—Amos, Hosea, Isaiah, and Micah—represent a new stage in the development of prophecy. While it was once thought that the Old Testament represented the earliest stage of language, serious reflection about life, and the prototype of religion, the past hundred years have enabled us to view Israel within the history of the ancient Near East and thus as part of a process—sociological, cultural, religious—of historical development. Ever since the discovery of sites and artifacts in Egypt and Mesopotamia a century ago, scholars have been at work demonstrating indeed that Israel was a child of her times, a culture among other cultures—and a late comer at that. At some points the comparison of literary and religious phenomena in the Near East led to a devaluation of the Old Testament as consisting of little more than stolen goods. More reasonable approaches to the comparative phenomena have led to the recognition that while Israel did indeed use many of the stories, religious objects and practices, and other material in common with her neighbors, the Old Testament witnesses reinterpreted and modified the material in order to witness to a different God. This assertion holds true for forms of speech, of architecture, of festivals; it holds true too for certain kinds of prophecy.

We know from the Old Testament itself that prophets were a class of functionaries among the Canaanites. King Ahab's wife Jezebel had "at her table" four hundred and fifty prophets of Baal and four hundred prophets of Asherah (1 Kings 18:19). When Elijah challenged this array of prophets to a contest on Mount Carmel, their activity betrayed the nature of their "prophecy": they shouted noises, danced around their altar, gashed themselves with swords until the blood gushed out, and raved on and on (1 Kings 18:26-29). Apparently all this activity was designed to effect by imitative magic a rain storm from their apparently dead god Baal. A similar kind of ecstatic behavior is attested in the story of Samuel's anointing of Saul to be king; one of the signs that the Lord has so anointed Saul is his meeting a band of prophets from Gibeathelohim who appear with "harp, tambourine, flute, and lyre before them, prophesying" (1 Sam. 10:1-8). In another story concerning Saul, the king and his messengers "prophesied"—their activity involved stripping off their clothes and lying naked (1 Sam. 19:18-24). Apart from this ecstatic behavior, no other activity is described in these texts as the function of prophets.

The closest parallel to the more common form of Old Testament prophecy has been found in the eighteenth century B.C. city of Mari, located in southern Mesopotamia and excavated from 1933–1956. The inhabitants of Mari were identified as Northwest Semites and thus related to the patriarchs of the Old Testament. Studies of some of the thousands of letters found at the site have revealed some striking similarities to Old Testament prophecy. Like Isaiah (Isa. 6) a man visiting his temple has a vision (or dream) in which he is instructed by the god to carry a message. Like Isaiah (6:8), Jeremiah (1:7), and Ezekiel (2:4), a man is "sent" by the god to relay the message. Like virtually all Old Testament prophets, messages from the men of Mari are addressed to a concrete situation. Like Gad and Nathan in David's court, the messengers direct support and challenge to the king in his rule. In fact, in the Mari letters all the prophetic words are directed to kings; before the writing prophets of the eighth century B.C. most Old Testament prophecy was addressed to the rulers. Thus the basic parallel between Mari and the Old Testament is that there appears a messenger of a god who, without being prepared and without initiative of his own, is sent with a specific address to other people. Surely there is a long and complicated prehistory of prophecy about which we know very little—a development which extends from the eighteenth to the eighth centuries B.C.

What stands out as decisive once again is the uniqueness of Israel's prophecy—not in terms of the forms but, as in almost all comparative phenomena, in the content. While the eighth century prophets of Israel and Judah spoke to kings, they were primarily sent by the Lord to address his will in the concrete situations of life to his chosen people. Those human words of Amos, Hosea, Isaiah, and Micah have their meaning and significance only because of the divine will which inspired and sent the prophets and because of the concrete situations they addressed with God's message.

Professor Bernhard Anderson dramatically describes this prophetic task as making "the eschatological shock of God's future effective in the present." At the same time these eighth century prophets reminded the people that the Lord had been at work in the crises of the past. The future and the past of God's dealing with his people come to bear on the present by God's own involvement in his relationships with his people. The author thus makes clear that Israelite prophecy has to do with a certain sense of history; such a view of past, present, and future distinguishes the prophets of the Old Testament from all known parallels in the ancient world, even those striking similarities from Mari.

Faithful to the intention and purpose of this series, Anderson presents a theology of the Old Testament prophets as evidenced in these eighth century spokesmen. Rather than treating each prophet independently, he treats all four thematically, thus highlighting in a unique way the distinctiveness of the "writing prophets" of Israel at this initial stage of their development. This treatment is strongly homiletical as well as theological and will serve as a valuable resource for preaching and teaching on any or all of these prophetic books.

Bernhard Anderson is Professor of Old Testament Theology at Princeton Theological Seminary. Author and editor of numerous books and articles, he is perhaps best known for his volume *Understanding the Old Testament* (now in its third edition) which is used in many colleges as a standard textbook on the history of Israel and the development of the Old Testament. In recent years Professor Anderson has offered specific courses and lectures on preaching from the Old Testament and thus brings to this series his established expertise in the field as well as his direct involvement with the questions of preaching the Word of God to audiences today.

Spring, 1978

FOSTER R. McCURLEY
Lutheran Theological Seminary at Philadelphia

To Joyce
Partner in Life and Ministry

INTRODUCTION

Christians should need no special urging to turn to the prophets of ancient Israel. Down through the centuries the witness of the prophets has been an essential ingredient of Christian theology, worship, and proclamation. Theologians have based their apologetic, or defense of Christian faith, in part on the argument that Old Testament prophecies are fulfilled in Jesus Christ. Worshipers have found themselves surrounded by cathedral art which portrays Jesus Christ flanked, on the one side, by the company of the prophets and, on the other, by the circle of the apostles. And today in Christian worship services the reading of a passage from prophets like Amos or Hosea, Isaiah or Micah, is prefaced by the announcement: "Hear the word of the Lord," or "Listen for the Word of God."

In early Christian proclamation Israel's prophets, including those with whom we are concerned in this study, were regarded as precursors of Jesus, the Messiah or Christ. In the Christian perspective, they pointed toward the denouement of the biblical story in Jesus' passion and resurrection, like John the Baptist in Grünewald's Eisenheim altar piece (Colmar, France), whose lean, boney finger points to the figure on the Cross. Accordingly, we frequently read in the New Testament that something was said or done in order that a word spoken by a prophet might be fulfilled. Luke gives a beautiful illustration of this futuristic or teleological view of prophecy in a post-resurrection story (Luke 24). Two bewildered disciples, so the story goes, were joined during their walk to Emmaus by a Stranger (Jesus unrecognized) who proceeded to explain to them that what had happened was "necessary" in God's unfolding plan and that the prophets, as well as other scriptural witnesses, had actually pointed to *himself* (Luke 24:25–27). As we well know, the theme of prophetic *anticipation* is a prominent aspect of Christian proclamation, especially in the season of Advent when familiar prophecies of Isaiah (Isa. 7:10–17; 9:2–7) or Micah (Mic. 5:2–4) are re-read and re-interpreted in the light of the Christ event.

The relation between Israel's scriptures and Jesus Christ, however, is two-directional: the movement is from the prophets to Jesus *and* from Jesus to the prophetic kerygma. The prophets not only "point to," they also "point out," that is, they proclaim the meaning of life *now* in relationship to the promises and demands of God. The double function of the prophetic word—teleological and kerygmatic—may be illustrated by our English words "indicate, indicator, indication." We say that clouds "indicate" rain in the sense that they point to or predict future weather developments. But we also say that a smile or a frown "indicates" something about a relationship in the present: approval or disapproval, favor or disfavor, love or anger. The words of the prophets are indications in this latter sense: they point out the meaning of life now in the immediacy of personal encounter and relationship with God.

Jesus himself has drawn our attention to this second—or perhaps we should say, primary—function of the prophetic word. On one occasion, according to the Gospel of Matthew, he was challenged about the propriety of having table fellowship with the riffraff of society: "tax collectors and sinners." He responded by saying that it is the sick, not those who are well, who need a physician; and he capped his remark with the imperative: "Go and learn what this word means: 'I desire mercy, and not sacrifice' " (Matt. 9:10–13; cf. 12:1–8). Here he appealed to his hearers to reexamine their behavior and prejudices by listening to the prophetic word found in Hosea 6:6—a passage that will engage our attention later on. According to the Gospel of Luke, Jesus' proclamation belonged squarely in the tradition of prophetic preaching about social justice, for he opened his ministry in his home town, Nazareth, by reading from the scroll of Isaiah (Luke 4:16–30):

> The Spirit of the Lord God is upon me,
>   because the Lord has anointed me
> to bring good tidings to the afflicted;
>   he has sent me to bind up the brokenhearted,
> to proclaim liberty to the captives,
>   and the opening of the prison to those who are bound;
> to proclaim the year of the Lord's favor . . .
>
> (Isa. 61:1–2a).

Jesus' imperative, "go and learn," sends us to the Old Testament to hear words of the prophets that cut incisively into the wounds of social life and bring to bear the therapy, or healing power, of divine judgment and grace. Christian churches are strongest when "the gift of prophecy" (1 Cor. 13:2) is not equated with knowledge of future mysteries but is a prophetic exposition of the meaning of life *now* in the immediacy and urgency of relationship with God. Such insight is not limited to special persons—those who are set apart by theological training and ordination to the ministry, or those who claim unusual charismatic powers. In a profound sense, all of the Lord's people should have the spirit of prophecy (cf. Num. 11:29), a contagion that is transferred to those under the influence of prophets like Amos, Hosea, Isaiah, and Micah. The prophetic gift becomes evident in the church whenever people boast not of their wisdom, power, or riches, but that they know Yahweh who practices faithfulness, justice, and righteousness in the earth (Jer. 9:23–24) and, in this personal knowledge, take a stand against whatever debases human dignity, oppresses the poor and helpless, and wantonly exploits our God-given natural resources.

Jesus' imperative, then, sends us beyond the context of the New Testament itself into the Scriptures of Israel which Christians call "The Old Testament." It is not enough to say that prophecy is "fulfilled" in the Christian gospel; we must also understand the prophetic word in its original situation in life. We must project ourselves into the times of the prophets (in this case the period of the eighth century B.C.) and read the prophetic message in the light of our historical understanding of the Bible. Martin Luther, though he lived long before the rise of modern critical study of the Bible, pointed the way. He wrote:[1]

> For if one would understand the prophecies, it is necessary that one know how things were in the land, how matters lay, what was in the mind of the people—what plans they had with respect to their neighbors, friends, and enemies—and especially what attitude they took in their country toward God and toward the prophet, whether they held to his word and worship or to idolatry.

There could hardly be a better definition of the task that lies before us.

And now, dear reader, a word of advice before we begin our

study of the eighth century prophets. No book about the prophets, especially a slender one like this, can possibly be a substitute for reading the prophetic literature itself. At various points along the way specific passages (listed in the index below) will be discussed, and you are urged to have at hand one or more of the following English translations:

Revised Standard Version, hereafter abbreviated as RSV—an ecumenical version approved by Protestant, Roman Catholic, and Eastern Orthodox representatives.

New English Bible, hereafter abbreviated as NEB—a translation into vigorous, idiomatic English.

New American Bible, hereafter abbreviated as NAB—a translation by a team of Roman Catholic scholars.

(Unless otherwise indicated, scriptural quotations will be from RSV.)

PERICOPE INDEX
(Passages Given Special Attention)

CHAPTER ONE

THE LION HAS ROARED

Across the lengthening distance of the years we can still sense the awesome reverberations of words spoken many centuries ago by four prophets of Israel: Amos and Hosea, Isaiah and Micah. The voice of prophecy, heard in the latter part of the eighth century B.C., was like the roar of a lion that pierced the noise of marketplaces and solemn assemblies, awakening people to a sober sense of historical reality and raising consciousness to a higher level. In the judgment of one historian of thought, Israel's prophets belonged to "the axial age of human history"—a time that brought about a profound change in human self-understanding over against the massive powers that depersonalize and dehumanize.[2]

The great prophets, beginning with Samuel, appeared at a time of transition within the movement of Israel's history: when the people determined to become a kingdom like other small nations of the ancient Near East (1 Sam. 8). The prophets were the successors to the "judges," the charismatic leaders of the former tribal confederacy. According to Amos, Yahweh performed a new act by raising up prophets to speak to Israel (Amos 2:11). Hosea declared that Yahweh "lashed" and "tore [his people] to shreds" through his words spoken by the prophets (Hos. 6:5, NEB). Isaiah's vision of divine transcendence constrained him to speak even though the people would not hear (Isa. 6:9–10). And Micah cried out against the injustices of society because he was a charismatic person, filled with the Spirit of God.

> But as for me, I am filled with power,
>> with the Spirit of Yahweh,*
>> and with justice and might,
> to declare to Jacob his transgression,
>> and to Israel his sin (Mic. 3:8).

*In translations the proper name "Yahweh" is used, rather than the substitute "the Lord" [Adonai].

1

THE HISTORICAL PARTICULARITY OF
THE PROPHETIC MESSAGE

Within the compass of a brief study how shall we proceed to understand the proclamation of the eighth century prophets? One approach would be to consider the four prophets individually, perhaps pairing Amos and Hosea, whose message was directed to north Israel (Ephraim) before the fall of Samaria in 721 B.C., and Isaiah and Micah, whose words were addressed to south Israel (Judah) in the latter years of the century (before 700 B.C.). This method would have the merit of displaying the individuality of each prophet and the distinctiveness of his message. The disadvantage of this approach is that repetition and overlapping would result. Furthermore, commentaries are available which treat the prophets individually and expound their writings chapter by chapter, and there is no need to rival or duplicate these works. Another approach is to consider the four prophets as a group—a prophetic quartet that sings the same themes. This, we believe, is a legitimate way to study these prophets; for despite differences in temperament, background, and theological accent they display an amazing consensus on the core of the prophetic message. As Johannes Lindblom, a Scandinavian Old Testament scholar, observes: "The central message was always the same; its application changed from time to time with changing historical circumstances."[3]

The danger of this approach, as Lindblom rightly points out, is that one attempts to force the prophets into the Procrustean bed of a theological or philosophical system. The prophets did not share a body of "right doctrine" (orthodoxy), nor was their message a deduction from a coherent fund of truths self-evident to reason. All attempts to systematize the message of the prophets are doomed to failure precisely because the words they spoke in concrete situations were laden with the "incarnate" power of the word of God, that is, a word that was directed into actual situations of human life. They shared a common core of preaching themes, but their preaching was always related to concrete life situations and to the particularities of human history.

So, if—in response to Jesus' imperative—we are to go and learn what the words of the eighth century prophets mean, we must allow ourselves to be drawn into the dramatic, living context of their preaching. It is theologically significant that each of the books that bears the name of an eighth century prophet has a superscription that relates the prophetic message to the political history of the times (Amos 1:1; Hos. 1:1; Isa. 1:1; Mic. 1:1). In the crowded fifty years between the time when Amos travelled from his home town in Tekoa to preach in the. northern city of Bethel and the last echo of the words of Isaiah in the city of Jerusalem (ca. 750–700 B.C.)—less than the span of a normal human life—seismic events shook the foundations of the ancient world and drew small nations, like Israel and Judah, into the vortex of international politics. The task of the eighth century prophets was to interpret these events in a dimension that transcended ordinary politics, and at the same time to proclaim "the word of the Lord" in concrete situations where people were living and dying, suffering and hoping.

THE POLITICS OF YAHWEH

The prophetic message then is inseparable from the world of politics, which is the world in which all of us live. In the eighth century B.C. the new political reality was the rise and expansion of Assyria. Assyria's first bid for world power had occurred about a century earlier, in the period of Elijah. At that time a group of small nations, including north Israel (Ephraim), formed an alliance for the purpose of stopping Assyrian aggression, and in the year 853 B.C. fought Assyria to a temporary standstill at Qarqar in Mesopotamia. The result was a breathing spell of a whole century, during which the kingdoms of Israel under Jeroboam II (786–746 B.C.) and of Judah under Uzziah or Azariah (783–742) achieved unprecedented economic prosperity and political stability. In both kingdoms, according to a vivid oracle of Amos (6:1–8), the comfortable, power-holding class of people felt "at ease in Zion" and "secure on the mount of Samaria," with no tinge of conscience about the inner ruin of society and no foreboding of the deluge that was about to come. But the complacent scene was soon to change. With the accession of the dynamic ruler, Tiglath-pileser III (745–727 B.C.), Assyria awoke from a century of political slumber and began to move relentlessly through the ancient Near East toward its ultimate goal: conquest of Egypt. [See chronological chart on next page.]

THE EIGHTH CENTURY PROPHETS
AND THEIR TIMES*

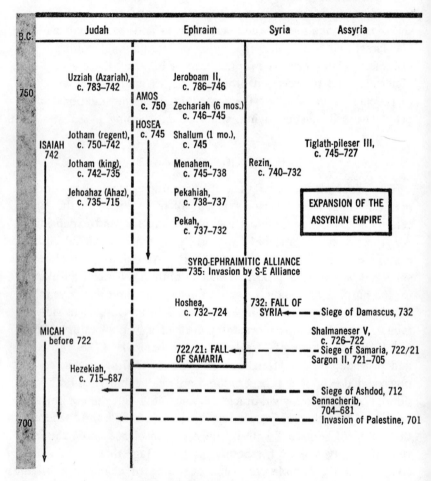

B.C.	PALESTINE		SYRIA & MESOPOTAMIA	
	Judah	Ephraim	Syria	Assyria
750	Uzziah (Azariah), c. 783–742	Jeroboam II, c. 786–746		
	AMOS c. 750	Zechariah (6 mos.) c. 746–745		
	HOSEA c. 745			
	Jotham (regent), c. 750–742	Shallum (1 mo.), c. 745		Tiglath-pileser III, c. 745–727
	ISAIAH 742			
	Jotham (king), c. 742–735	Menahem, c. 745–738	Rezin, c. 740–732	
	Jehoahaz (Ahaz), c. 735–715	Pekahiah, c. 738–737		EXPANSION OF THE ASSYRIAN EMPIRE
		Pekah, c. 737–732		
		SYRO-EPHRAIMITIC ALLIANCE 735: Invasion by S-E Alliance		
		Hoshea, c. 732–724	732: FALL OF SYRIA	Siege of Damascus, 732
	MICAH before 722	722/21: FALL OF SAMARIA		Shalmaneser V, c. 726–722 Siege of Samaria, 722/21 Sargon II, 721–705
	Hezekiah, c. 715–687			Siege of Ashdod, 712 Sennacherib, 704–681
700				Invasion of Palestine, 701

*Adapted from Chronological Chart in *Understanding the Old Testament* by Bernhard W. Anderson, third edition (Englewood Cliffs, N.J.: Prentice-Hall, 1975), pp. 603–604. Reprinted by permission of Prentice-Hall, Inc.

When Amos preached in Bethel, the international storm was only a cloud on the horizon, scarcely visible. He perceived, however, that in the age-old game of power politics, a society rotting with injustice from within was vulnerable to attack from without. In a short time the tempest broke with military fury, spreading quickly across the land of Palestine. In the second half of the eighth century B.C., the prophetic message was punctuated by three major political crises.

1. 735–732 B.C. (See Hosea 5:8–14; Isaiah 7:1–17)
   Another "stop Assyria" movement was led by two small nations, Syria and Ephraim, who attempted to force Judah into the coalition.
   Result: Tiglath-pileser's army intervened and Damascus, capital of Syria, fell in 732 B.C.

2. 724–721 B.C. (See Hosea 8:1–10; Isaiah 10:5–19; Micah 1:2–7)
   Tiglath-pileser's death in 727 B.C. prompted the king of Ephraim to revolt and withhold tribute. The successor to the Assyrian throne, Shalmanezer V (726–722 B.C.), laid siege to Samaria, capital of Ephraim.
   Result: Sargon II (721–705 B.C.), the next Assyrian monarch, finished the conquest of Samaria and carried many Israelites into exile.

3. 712–701 B.C. (See Isaiah 20; Micah 1:10–16; Isaiah 1:4–9)
   Revolt against Assyria broke out again, initially centered in the Gaza strip but spreading elsewhere in the empire. Sargon's successor, Sennacherib, marched triumphantly through Palestine and decisively quelled the rebellion.
   Result: After devastating much of Judah and surrounding Jerusalem, the Assyrian army returned home and there was respite for a while.

Had there been newspapers in those days, these are the events that probably would have made the headlines.[4] Indeed, the events are firmly recorded in Israel's historical annals, as we know from 2 Kings 15—20 where Tiglath-pileser (Pul) is mentioned. The prophets, however, were not news reporters or archivists. They were commentators on the religious meaning these political events had for people caught in the tragic grip of historical and social forces beyond their control. They saw what was happening *sub specie aeternitatis,* "under the view of Eternity," or, better, under the view of the eternal God, Yahweh, whose purpose for Israel—and the world—was disclosed in traditions reaching back to crucial experiences of the past, preeminently the exodus from Egypt and the covenant at Sinai.

In this respect, the prophets were concerned primarily with the people, especially those who were victims of the power structure of society, the "nobodies" whom everybody but the God of Israel had forgotten.   A great deal of literature has been preserved from the ancient past which speaks on behalf of kings, aristocracy, or the economically powerful.   But the words of the prophets have survived in written form as a unique testimony to concern for the poor, the oppressed, the legally helpless—those whose cries of suffering are heard only by God (cf. Exod. 3:7–9!).   As Abraham Heschel observed, prophecy is the voice God has lent to the silent agony of mankind.

THE METAPHOR OF THE LION

The keynote of the prophetic message is heard when we open the first book in the sequence of eighth century prophets, namely, Amos. The ominous roar of a lion sounds forth from Zion (Jerusalem), sending a shudder of terror through shepherds and flocks far to the north, even on the top of Mount Carmel (Amos 1:2).   The roar, however, is not that of the Assyrian lion advancing from his Mesopotamian lair to seize his political prey.   Rather, in a daring poetic metaphor, Yahweh is the Lion who crouches to leap on his quarry and whose voice roars in judgment.

The theological introduction to the Book of Amos carries overtones that reverberate beyond the specific situation of Amos' preaching in Bethel.   The reference to Zion (the place of the Davidic-Solomonic temple), and the similarity of the poetic formulation to other prophetic passages (e.g., Joel 3:16), seem to indicate that the opening verse was added when Amos' message, originally proclaimed in the North, was edited for use in the southern kingdom of Judah. Nevertheless, the lion metaphor belongs authentically to Amos' proclamation, as is evident from the important passage in Amos 3:3–8, which is the best place to begin our study.

To understand the force of prophetic preaching in Amos 3:3–8 (and this applies to any passage from prophetic books), two things must be considered: a) the literary form and setting in life, and b) the function of the literary unit in its present context. Let us consider both matters briefly.

First of all, the passage is a literary unit or "pericope," to use a Greek word which suggests that one can cut around the passage and lift it out without damaging its integrity. As a literary unit, it has its own beginning and ending, and seems to be complete in itself. Moreover, this unit belongs to a literary genre that presupposes a particular setting in life, namely, the situation in which wisdom teachers engaged in "disputation," or instruction carried out by rhetorical questions and illustrations based on ordinary human experience. A teacher might "dispute":

> Do two walk together unless they have made an appointment?
> Does a lion roar in the forest when he has no prey?
>
> (Amos 3:3–4a)

Clearly, people do not travel together unless they have agreed in advance on a place and time of meeting. To use another illustration, a bird does not fall into a trap unless the catch has been set (3:5). The wisdom teacher insists that in the orderly sphere of daily experience, events do not happen haphazardly, without rhyme or reason.

Using this literary form, Amos also invites his hearers to agree that in an orderly world a particular consequence has its correlative cause. Notice, however, that in verse 6 his "disputation" takes an unexpected turn: if disaster befalls a city, has not Yahweh been at work? The argument is *ad hominem* and therefore is not intended to make the sweeping generalization that all disasters (earthquakes, floods, and other natural catastrophes) are the work of God. Moving through a series of illustrations the passage reaches its target in verse 8. Here we learn that the prophetic compulsion to speak is motivated ("caused") by something prior: Yahweh, the Lion, has roared! (Verse 7, which breaks the poetic pattern and introduces a general claim about prophecy may be a later expansion.) In other words, one evidence—in fact, the supreme evidence—that this is God's orderly world, not a world ruled by chance or brute power, is that Yahweh has spoken and the reflex is the speaking of a prophet.

> The lion has roared—who will not fear?
> The Lord God has spoken—who will not prophesy? (Amos 3:8)

In the second place, this distinct literary unit functions in a context that is also important for understanding the prophetic proclamation. Notice that this unit is surrounded by passages that deal, on the one hand, with divine election and, on the other, with divine rejection. In this context, the theme of "action and consequence" (found in the disputation unit 3:3–8) is emphasized. In both cases the key word is "therefore." The initial utterance, which begins with the catchword "Hear," announces that Yahweh's act of election has consequences: "You only have I known . . . therefore . . ." (3:2). Moreover, the people's behavior has consequences: "They do not know how to do right . . . therefore . . ." (3:10–11). We begin to sense that it is the ominous "therefore" of God's purpose that provides the inescapable link between action and consequence and that discloses the meaning of the historical events that impinge upon Israel, the people of his choice.

GOD'S PRESENCE IN THE WORLD

Only a poet would dare to speak of God metaphorically as a Lion or, as in the case of Francis Thompson, a "Hound of Heaven" who relentlessly pursues his quarry "down the nights and down the days." Elsewhere biblical poets draw their imagery from family relationships (father, mother, kinsman) or from the royal court (king, judge, shepherd). But here the poet boldly takes his cue from the predatory forest: Yahweh is the roaring Lion, King of the beasts! The lion metaphor has two aspects, each of which is essential for understanding the message of eighth century prophets.

First, what motivated—indeed, compelled—the prophets to speak was the inescapable presence of the holy God in the world. We are apt to use quiet, soothing adjectives to describe God's presence in our midst; but the poets of Israel, both prophets and psalmists, used disturbing language. "The Lord, the Most High, is terrible" (Ps. 47:2). "Great is the Lord, and greatly to be praised; he is to be feared above all gods" (Ps. 96:4). "Let them praise thy great and terrible name" (Ps. 99:3). Such testimonies, characteristic of

Israel's worship, could be expanded easily. Yahweh is the Holy One in the midst of Israel—a theme that runs through the preaching of all the eighth century prophets—and this belief poses the question of how a people can and should live in the presence of God. We are reminded in the New Testament that "it is a fearful thing to fall into the hands of the living God" (Heb. 10:31).

Secondly, the lion metaphor suggests, shockingly, that God's prey is his own people. Hosea, who preached in the northern kingdom not long after Amos' appearance in Bethel, did not hesitate to draw out the brutal implications of the poetic imagery. In his poetic language Yahweh, the God of Israel, says:

> I will be like a lion to Ephraim,
>> and like a young lion to the house of Judah.
> I, even I, will rend and go away,
>> I will carry off, and none shall rescue (Hos. 5:14; cf. 13:7–8).

Of course, Hosea also used other poetic imagery (husband-wife, father-son), but the lion language should not be ignored. The prophets declared that people could not know God as a "friend" until they first knew him as an "enemy"—to recall something a philosopher (A. N. Whitehead) once said.

This is an amazing proclamation! There is hardly anything like it in the religions of the ancient world, and it was certainly a new element in the history of Israel's worship. Basic to Israelite faith, as we learn from the prophets themselves, was the conviction that Yahweh had chosen Israel to be his own people and that with them he had entered into a close, personal relationship. "You only have I known of all the families of the earth . . ." (Amos 3:2); "It was I who knew you in the wilderness . . ." (Hos. 13:5). "Sons have I reared and brought up . . ." (Isa. 1:2). The people fervently believed that Yahweh is "with us" (Amos 3:2), present "in our midst" (Hos. 11:9; Mic. 3:11b), and "our God" (the God of Israel). These convictions, however, were popularly understood by both priests and people to mean that Yahweh is on "our side," that he is "our God" in a possessive sense, and hence that he supports *our* way of life, upholds *our* values, and protects *our* interests. The radically new message of the eighth century prophets was that divine election does not exclude divine rejection. To live in the presence of

Yahweh, the Holy One, is to experience his inescapable judgment which searches the innermost heart and exposes the subtlest forms of social oppression. In view of the incompatibility of human ways with God's righteousness, the prophets raised the question as to whether Israel could stand in his holy presence on the day of his appearance.

In the chapters that follow, we shall explore the themes that were central to the prophetic message and that found varied expression in changing circumstances. It is important to begin, however, with the recognition that the prophetic proclamation was based on the fundamental awareness of God's awesome presence in the midst of Israel and in the world. The task of prophetic preaching was to translate God's presence into human speech. As Abraham Heschel observed in his unexcelled exposition of the prophetic perspective, the prophets of Israel spoke in poetic language, seeking to express more than ordinary language can convey, in order that "the invisible God becomes audible."[5] To see the invisible God is more than can be expected under the conditions of mortal existence (cf. Exod. 33:20–23). But the creative accomplishment of prophets like Amos and Hosea, Isaiah and Micah, was to allow the presence of God to become vocal in human language, so that the roar of the Lion might be heard. And, in some degree, that is what happens when any preaching is truly prophetic in spirit.

CHAPTER TWO

THE SHOCK OF GOD'S FUTURE

An intense awareness of the presence of God in the world prompted the prophets to conjugate the verbs of human existence—past, present, and future—in a new way. Some people turn to the past with religious nostalgia, hoping to recover the "good old days" or the "old time religion"; others believe that the most important tense religiously is the present, which one should seize with existential passion. Even a cursory reading of the eighth century prophets, however, shows that they were fiercely obsessed with the future. They perceived that something startlingly new, shockingly unexpected, was shaping up on the horizon of tomorrow or the day after, and their future insight motivated them to alert people to the urgency of the present and to recall a past that had been all but forgotten.

The prophets had little to say about the events of an individual's life as it moves from the mystery of birth through various times of transition to the inevitable terminus of death—and the intimations of unbroken fellowship with God beyond (cf. Ps. 73:23-26). Rather, they turned outward from the private realm of the individual heart to the public events that were occurring, or about to occur, on the world scene, events that would have an inescapable impact on the nations and particularly on Israel, the people of God. The details of the future were of no special interest to them, for the prophets were not clairvoyants who looked into a crystal ball or political soothsayers like those consulted by kings before a battle. They were certain, however, that in the near future historical catastrophe would shake the world of the nations, bringing about profound changes in people's lives and a new understanding of reality.

In the twentieth century it may be possible for us to understand, at least in some degree, the prophetic sense of time. Various secular thinkers—ecologists, political scientists, and other concerned special-ists—have raised the question as to whether the earth can support our present lifestyle and have warned of a catastrophic future which will bring the end sooner than we think.   In our period, too, the issue is whether the "future shock" is sufficient to awaken people to the urgency of the present and to the recovery of our rootage in the past.

There is, however, a major difference between the prophetic message and modern secular thought.   The prophets proclaimed that the coming turn of historical events would be the occasion for an encounter with God, who would manifest his historical presence in a new way, indeed, a way that was quite different from anything experienced before.   Hence, the shock of the future, whose reverbera-tions were felt in the present, was really an "eschatological shock," for Yahweh's coming on the horizon of the future introduced the time of the end, especially for Israel.   If the future held this mean-ing—God's coming to judge his people and the nations—then the present should be inescapably urgent.   It is no time for business as usual, or for the ordinary services of religion.   Rather, as Amos pointed out, the present is a time for critical and penitent reappraisal of a people's whole life: "Prepare to meet your God, O Israel!" (Amos 4:12).

THE END HAS COME!

An excellent way to plunge into this dynamic theme of prophetic proclamation is to turn to Amos' visions which provide the literary framework of chapters 7—9, and especially the fourth vision which contains Yahweh's announcement that "the end has come upon my people Israel" (8:1–3).   Here the eschatological urgency of Amos' message is expressed by using a conventional literary form: a vision that presents a dialogue between Yahweh and his prophet.

The vision is cast into a threefold sequence: a) Yahweh opens the dialogue with a question: "What do you see?"   b) The prophet answers by focusing on an object of the everyday world: "I see a basket. . . ." And c) Yahweh responds by commending him for his observation but raising his perception to a higher level of meaning. The same dialogic structure is found in Amos' vision of the plumbline

(Amos 7:7–9) and in Jeremiah's visions of the almond rod or the boiling pot (Jer. 1:11–14).

Visions and dreams often need to be decoded, as in the case of the visions found in later apocalyptic literature (e.g., Dan. 2). But in this case the interpretation is given in the context of the vision. The object at the center of attention is a basket of summer fruit, possibly an offering brought to the sanctuary for the celebration of the Fall Festival of Ingathering (New Year's) after the summer harvest. Normally, such a basket of fruit would signify divine blessing and the renewal of hope that comes with the rotation of the seasons. But the Hebrew word for "summer fruit" (*qayiṣ*), by associative assonance, triggers another word, "end" (*qēṣ*). Suddenly the meaning of the vision, in which Yahweh is the primary speaker, becomes all too clear. The basket of "ripe summer fruit," as NEB translates, indicates that "the time is ripe" for Israel. Even though outwardly Israelite society seemed prosperous and secure, the reality of the end was already present, as indicated by the Hebrew verbal form (prophetic perfect): "The end has come" (cf. the usage of the word *qēṣ*, "end," in the introduction to the Flood Story [Gen. 6:13] and in Ezekiel's prophecy [Ezek. 7:1–9]). This devastating event, as we learn from the vision itself, will not be the expression of historical fate but of Yahweh's encounter with his people: "I will never again pass them by." And the divine-human encounter will be so upsetting that the songs of joy and thanksgiving, appropriate at the harvest festival, will be converted into mourning and lamentation.

This literary unit has its own distinctive form and content, but it now functions in a larger literary context. Like a magnet, the vision has drawn to it several poetic units that elaborate its meaning: the coming day of judgment. Those who trample on the poor and needy face a time of general mourning, for Yahweh "will never forget any of their deeds" (8:4–8). On that day there will be darkness at high noon and festal songs will be turned into lamentation (8:9–10). It will be a time of spiritual famine when the word of Yahweh is no longer heard (8:11–12), and when fair virgins and young men will faint for thirst (8:13–14).

The theme of the actuality of the end also resounds in other literary contexts of prophecy. Assuming the role of a mourner at a funeral, Amos pronounces a dirge over "the Virgin Israel" who, though living, has actually collapsed (5:1–2). Appropriately the poetry is cast in the 3/2 rhythm of lament used by mourners who follow the bier to the grave:

> She is fállen nevermore to ríse,
> the Vírgin Iśrael;
> Próstrate she lieś on her soíl,
> nó one to uplíft her.
>   [Author's translation]

The lament is appropriately supplemented by the wailing cry of mourners, *hôy,* "alas" (often translated "woe"), in which the prophet considers the various signs of *rigor mortis* in the body of Israel (Amos 5:18–20; 6:1–7; see also Isa. 5:8–23; 10:1–4). Israel's case is terminal, like that of a person who suffers from incurable cancer and knows that the days are numbered.

The greatest theological problem faced by the prophets arose out of a cardinal conviction that is still fundamental and precious in religious life and worship: "God is with us" (the meaning of the word "Immanuel" in Isa. 7:14). People who thronged to the temple of Bethel in the North or Jerusalem in the South believed, as do many modern worshipers, that God was "with them" (Amos 5:14b). As Micah observed (Mic. 3:11b), they "leaned" (relied) on Yahweh and said,

> Is not Yahweh in the midst of us?
> No evil shall come upon us.

Faith in God meant faith in the future. Since God was with his people, endorsing their values and assuring them of a glorious future, the future was only an extension of the present—a fulfillment of present plans and a confirmation of present lifestyle. According to a familiar passage in the prophecy of Amos, which may reflect the old tradition of God's Holy War on behalf of his people, they expected that the coming "Day of Yahweh" would be "light" (Amos 5:18), that is, it would entail victory, prosperity, and welfare.

The prophets insisted, however, that there is no smooth, straight-line continuity from the present into the future. Rather, in the purpose of God, there must be a sharp discontinuity, a catastrophic break. The old world with its social injustices, its established structures, its false lifestyle had to come to an abrupt end.   Accordingly, the prophetic message shattered and reversed popular expectations. Amos proclaimed that the Day of Yahweh would be, paradoxically, a day of darkness with no sign of light, as though one were fleeing from a lion only to be confronted by a bear, or took refuge in a house where, exhausted, the fugitive leaned a hand against a wall, only to be bitten by a serpent (Amos 5:18–20).   In a similar vein Isaiah proclaimed that the coming Day would be the negation of all cultural values and splendor, a time when people would flee to caves in the rock before the inescapable presence of Yahweh (Isa. 2:6–21).   In short, God's future is not our human future.   On the contrary, the imminence of his coming out of the future introduces into the present such an eschatological shock that present plans, behavior, and style of life are called into question.

THE STORM OF GOD

The prophets of the eighth century believed that God's coming to judge his people was inseparably related to the international storm that was brewing ominously on the horizon.   They seemed to have a strangely ambivalent attitude toward the ever-changing political scene.   On the one hand, they scorned *Realpolitik* which tolerated the atrocities of war and led to excesses of power (see the oracles against the nations in Amos 1:3—2:3; Isa. 13:1—23:18).   They chided the leaders of Israel and Judah for panicking in the face of massive political forces and for the "political promiscuity" (Heschel) evident in flitting from one great power to another in an attempt to purchase security through military alliance (e.g., Hos. 7:11; Isa. 20). Israel's role, they insisted, was not to play the game of power politics. On the other hand, the prophets kept their ears to the ground, listening for every significant tremor on the political scene, for they perceived that at the depth of the political crisis Yahweh was present, in judgment and in mercy.

In Amos' time the political shape of the future was not clear.   It was sufficient for him to announce that "an adversary" would surround the land (Amos 3:11) or that Yahweh would "raise up a nation" to dominate the entire extent of Israelite territory (Amos 6:14).   A few years later, however, the Assyrian war-machine was rolling and Hosea, during the crisis of the Syro-Ephraimitic War (Hos. 5:8–14), referred specifically to the folly of placating the Assyrian king's favor (5:13). And not long afterward Isaiah and Micah presented vivid descriptions of the routes of the Assyrian invasion and the terror that filled the hearts of those in the path of the advance (Isa. 10:27d–32; Mic. 1:10–15). [See chronological chart, p. 4.]

These prophets viewed the international crisis as "the storm of Yahweh," to use an expression from Jeremiah (23:19). With every rumor from the North they perceived that the storm of God was coming toward the land of Israel closer and closer, and they regarded themselves as watchmen whose duty it was to alert the people to the urgency of the present. Most people then, as today, attempted to hide their heads in the sand, ostrichlike, and wait for the crisis to pass. The burden of prophetic preaching, however, was that in this world there is no hiding place from God, whose holy presence and searching judgment are inescapable (cf. Ps. 139:7–12). This is the theme of the last of Amos' visions (9:1–4). Significantly, the vision occurs in the temple, the place where fugitives from a pursuer sought sanctuary at the altar. But not even the sanctities of religion offered refuge; for Amos saw Yahweh himself standing beside the altar and giving the command to bring down the whole temple structure on the heads of the people. And it became clear that there is no hiding place, whether in the depths or the heights, from the judgment of God.

> Though they dig into Sheol,
>   from there shall my hand take them;
> Though they climb up to heaven,
>   from there I will bring them down (Amos 9:2).

It was difficult for the message of divine judgment to be heard in the northern kingdom, whose religious traditions reached back to the great patriarch, Jacob, who was regarded as the originator of Israelite worship at Bethel (Hos. 12:4; cf. Gen. 28:10–17; 35:5–8). The priest Amaziah reported to King Jeroboam that Amos had conspired against the throne, that the land could not tolerate his words; he warned Amos to go back to his home in the south, for Bethel "is the king's sanctuary and it is a temple of the kingdom" (Amos 7:10–

13). It was equally difficult for Isaiah to proclaim the message of divine judgment in the south, in Judah, for there the Jerusalem temple was regarded as the sanctuary that Yahweh had chosen and the Davidic king was held to be "the son of God," bound to Yahweh in a special covenant relationship (2 Sam. 7:11b–16; Pss. 89, 132). Nevertheless, Isaiah dared to say that Jerusalem would not escape the storm of God's judgment. Yahweh was performing his "strange work" on Mount Zion (Isa. 28:21).

The inescapable judgment of God is also the subject of a poem in which Isaiah portrays Yahweh speaking to the Assyrian dictator, though we are left to guess his identity (Tiglath-pileser III? Sargon II?). The poem falls into two major sections, separated by a prose summary (10:12) which announces the change that will occur when Yahweh has "finished his work on Mount Zion and Jerusalem."

A. 10:5–11. The first part develops the theme that the Assyrian is the instrument of the divine purpose—"the rod of Yahweh's anger." To be sure, the monarch does not realize this, but vainly supposes that he is acting only in his own political might and to fulfill his own military plan.

Transition (10:12)

B. 10:13–19. The second part announces that when Yahweh has finished his "strange work" on Mount Zion, he will shatter the presumption of the Assyrian who supposes that he is directing history. The Assyrian political ambition has a temporary function in "the politics of God," but the Assyrian flood, destructive as it is, cannot escape the contouring banks of God's purpose.

Meanwhile, the question for the people of Judah was what the international storm meant for faith's understanding in the present. Psalm 46, with its climactic word "Be still and know that I am God," belongs in this kind of life situation.

THE THERAPY OF CATASTROPHE

The proclamation of the eighth century prophets at times seems to be unbearably severe. Is it possible that the coming of God toward his people means the surrender of everything—security, confidence, even faith in the future? Abraham once was put to this test, according to the unforgettable story in Genesis 22, and the prophets seem to suggest that the people Israel were on the verge of going through such an experience again. It is no wonder that the literature of the prophets, in its final editing, was lightened up now and then with passages of hope and doxologies designed to make the difficult message more palatable for ancient (and modern) worship! It is generally believed, for instance, that the conclusion to the Book of Amos (9:11–15), with its sudden affirmative note, is a later expansion.

It would be wrong to suppose, however, that intimations or promises of hope were extraneous to the prophetic message, making it necessary for later editors to round out the picture with the announcement that, as in a good story, everyone lived happily ever afterward. The error in this view is the notion that divine judgment is the antithesis of divine grace, or that threats of doom are unrelated to possibilities of renewal. At the level of strict logic these things may seem contradictory, but the sharp alternative hardly does justice to the depths of human experience. As we know from situations close at hand, a person who is confronted with a debilitating bodily handicap or even a terminal illness may find in the situation an unexpected release of new powers. And, as the prophets of Israel said in various ways, a people confronted with the reality of death in the political sphere may find in the crisis the grace to recover its identity and its vitality. The shock treatment of historical catastrophe belongs to divine therapy.

The theme of Israel's death is the subject of a moving poem in Hosea 13:1–16. Some commentators maintain that the poem reflects the political situation in the northern kingdom a few years before the Assyrian conquest of Samaria—a time when, in the unpredictable game of politics, Ephraim's national optimism flared up again, perhaps as the result of some new sign of support from Egypt (see 13:10–11, 15a). This would locate the passage in the hectic years just before the fall of Samaria in 721 B.C. (so H. W. Wolff, *Hosea,* p. 224). In this political setting the prophet declared that Ephraim had already died even though there were still signs of bodily activity, and that "the wages of sin" (i.e., rebellion against God) was death, a motif recapitulated in Romans 6:23.

The poem may be divided into four units, each of which elaborates the theme of Israel's death.

A. God's accusation and announcement of judgment (13:1–3)
B. Israel's history of failure and its consequences (13:4–8)
C. The folly of trusting in political leaders (13:9–11)
D. The verdict of death (13:12–16)

There was a time, so we hear in the first movement of the poem, when Ephraim was preeminent among the tribes of Israel—perhaps a recollection of the time when the Ephraimite Joshua rallied the people to loyalty to the covenant (Josh. 24:14–15). But something happened: the people Ephraim (northern kingdom) became guilty of Baal-worship and "died," that is, they yielded to the gods of culture and adopted the lifestyle of the Canaanite religion represented by the fertility god (Baal) and his female counterpart. Therefore, they will evaporate like the morning mist or be blown away like chaff, for the character of a people is shaped by the objects of its worship (cf. Jer. 2:5).

The second movement of the poem (13:4–8) brings us to the heart of the problem: amnesia.

> I am Yahweh your God from the land of Egypt.
> > You know no God but me,
> > and besides me there is no savior.
> It was I who knew you in the wilderness,
> > in the land of drought.
> But when they had fed to the full, they were filled,
> > and their heart was lifted up;
> Therefore they forgot me (Hos. 13:4–6).

Israel's identity as a people was given in the story: Yahweh brought them out of Egypt, "knew" (NEB "cared for") them in the wilderness, and led them into the land. *But* in times of security and prosperity they "forgot" Yahweh, which was to forget the whole story that gave them identity and vocation as a people. Here Hosea does not speak about ordinary forgetfulness—doing something absent-mindedly or inadvertently. Rather, to forget Yahweh is an act of the will: a turning away from loyalty to the liberating God of the exodus, and at the same time a turning to another loyalty, the Baal who promised to bestow the meaning and blessing of life through a completely different story.

Do not underestimate the seductive power of the Baal *mythos*.

Even today it offers the view that human beings find the meaning of life in the rhythms of the natural world—the eternal return of the seasons, the mystery of fertility, the vitality of sex. Hosea does not completely repudiate Canaanite naturalism. He only insists that Yahweh has come to "know" Israel in a different way: through marvellous events that freed slaves and made them a people, with a future and a vocation (Hos. 13:4–5). How then could emancipated slaves ever forget that story—all that it meant, and all that it called for? The divine reaction is expressed in poetic language akin to that of Amos. Israel's encounter with Yahweh will be like facing a predatory beast of the forest, such as a lion, a leopard, or a bear (13:8). Nothing beautiful and sentimental about this religious experience! Nevertheless, Israel should know that they are not facing a strange, unknown God. The God who comes to judge is none other than the One whom they knew at the first as the Liberator and Savior.

The next section (13:9–11) indicates in even stronger terms that Israel's encounter with God in the historical arena will be ominously final. Indeed, the sentence in verse 9 probably should be translated: "I have destroyed you, O Israel!" (so NEB), a Hebrew "prophetic perfect" showing that the reality and certainty of the future is already felt in the present. No political panaceas are effective, not even the institution of kingship which the people once adopted in a time of desperation (1 Sam. 8), for the problem, as Hosea sees it, lies in the "heart" (the Hebrew term refers not to the center of emotions but to the mind and will). Something "irrational" has been at work: a "harlotrous spirit" (Hos. 5:4) has seized the people and led them astray into bondage to another loyalty, another story of salvation, another god. Only the most radical surgery can deal with this sickness unto death.

THE STING OF DEATH

The theme of death, which resounds through the individual strophes of the poem (Hos. 13:3, 7–8, 9, 14, 15–16), reaches its climax in the final section (13:12–16). Apparently the poet was influenced by Canaanite mythology in which the divine being Death (*Môt*) is portrayed as the enemy of Baal, Lord of storm and fertility. Hosea, however, regards Death as a power which Yahweh controls and addresses:

> O Death, where are your plagues?
> O Sheol, where is your destruction?

These words, with their mythological overtones, are quoted by Paul in 1 Corinthians 15:55, in the context of the proclamation that Death, "the last enemy" (1 Cor. 15:26), has been overcome through God's victory in Jesus Christ. But in Hosea's poem the words have a different meaning. In the immediate context (13:13) we find a striking figure of speech: Ephraim is compared to a fetus in the womb—a child mature enough to be born; but this "unwise son" refuses to go through the opening that leads to creative life! Israel's death, according to the prophet, resulted from both the people's congenital refusal to respond to the creative opportunity and from Yahweh's summons to Death to bring the final judgment upon a still-born infant.

This poem, with its powerful poetic imagery, should not be isolated from other aspects of the prophetic message. Yahweh's address to Death is concluded with the word: "compassion is hid from my eyes" (end of v. 14). This is not Yahweh's last word, however, as we find in another poem of Hosea (Hos. 11), to which we shall turn later. Nevertheless, it is important to feel the ominous poetic impact of this language, without trying to blunt its sharp edges or soften its severity. The language of prophetic preaching is often brutally harsh precisely because the prophets were overwhelmed by the gravity of the human situation. When the people have forgotten their past and the story which gave them identity and vocation, how can memory be restored without shock treatment? When the people are in bondage to a "god" or idol that falsely promises ultimate meaning, how can their chains be broken so that they may find freedom in the service of the God who is Lord of creation and history? These questions are as pertinent today as in the days of the eighth century prophets, even though Christian proclamation may use other literary forms.

If we are disturbed by the prophetic language, it is as it should be if the "word of God" is truly surgical and healing. As we are reminded in the New Testament: "The word of God is living and active, sharper than any two-edged sword . . . discerning the thoughts and intentions of the heart.   And before Him no creature is hidden, but all are open and laid bare to the eyes of him with whom we have to do" (Heb. 4:12–13).   The task of the prophets' preaching was to stir up a tumult in the human heart by speaking with such force that their words, through which God's word was mediated, could pierce illusions, shatter complacency, destroy false securities, challenge injustice, and raise the level of human consciousness.

In summary, the proper place to begin to understand the prophetic proclamation is with their sense of time, and particularly their awareness of the relation of the future to the present.   The eighth century prophets perceived that a storm was coming—"the east wind, the wind of Yahweh . . . rising from the wilderness," as Hosea said (Hos. 13:15).   As messengers of God, their task was to make the eschatological shock of God's future effective in the present, so that Israel—the people of God—might recover their identity and their vocation and so that possibly, in the incalculable grace of God, there might be a transition from death to life.

CHAPTER THREE

TURNING AWAY AND TURNING AROUND

The eighth century prophets, as we have seen, looked toward God's tomorrow for the purpose of accentuating the urgency of today. Each in his own way sounded the call that was heard in authentic services of worship: "O that *today* you would hearken to his voice!" (Ps. 95:7b; echoed in Heb. 3:7; 4:7). In the crises of their times they announced that people were being given a last chance to amend their ways. In this respect they were precursors of Jesus who opened his ministry in Galilee with the proclamation: "The time is fulfilled, and the kingdom of God is at hand; repent, and believe in the gospel!" (Mark 1:14–15).

One of the fundamental themes of prophetic preaching is "returning to God," that is, a conversion of the will to covenant relationship with Yahweh and all that such a reorientation demands in social relations. In Hebrew the key verb is *šûb*, often translated as "return"; for instance: "You did not return to me" (Amos 4:4–13); "Return, O Israel, to Yahweh your God" (Hos. 14:1); or "A remnant will return . . . to the Mighty God" (Isa. 10:21). Think also of the symbolic name of Isaiah's son, Shear-yashub, which means "A remnant shall return" (Isa. 7:3–4). The verb occurs many times in the Old Testament (more than 1000), but the importance of the theme of "returning" cannot be measured by the number of times it is used by a particular prophet.

When used theologically, the verb often indicates a motion in a certain direction, though the motion may be reversible. Generally speaking, the verb in its various modulations may have two senses: a) It may describe a motion of turning away from the direction in which one should be going. In this sense, sin is "apostasy, defection, faithlessness" (*mᵉšûbâ*, Hos. 14:4), that is, turning away from relationship with God.   b) Alternatively, it may describe a motion of turning about—a return to the way in which one was going prior to turning away. In this sense, repentance means redirection or reorientation to the relationship of faith.   Interestingly, the verb often has the concrete geographical meaning of returning to a point of departure, as when Israel, in the time of divine judgment, will "return to Egypt" (Hos. 11:5) or when, in a time of divine blessing, Israel will return to her land from which she was exiled (Jer. 31:21).   But even in these cases the metaphorical meaning prevails: Israel, like a prodigal son, defects from a relationship (leaves home) but is restored to that relationship (returns home).   It is on this positive note of "homecoming" that the prophecy of Hosea concludes (Hos. 14:1–8).

THE BONDAGE OF THE WILL

It is striking that the prophets of the eighth century do not begin their preaching with a call to repentance or "return to Yahweh." Modern preachers sometimes suppose that amendment of life is simply a matter of decision, like making New Year's resolutions to do better in the future.   The prophets, however, spoke to life situations in which people were stubbornly set in their ways, resolutely determined to follow a course leading to inevitable disaster.   In tones of bewilderment and consternation they accused the people of refusing to repent.   Israelites seemed to be trapped in bondage to a style of life from which they could not free themselves: "Their deeds will not permit them to return to their God" (Hos. 5:4).   In Hosea's magnificent poem that portrays Israel as a prodigal son (Hos. 11), Yahweh's word is: "My people are bent on turning from me" (v. 7a). Isaiah sounds the same note: "In returning and rest you shall be saved . . . but *you would not*" (Isa. 30:15).

The prophetic message reflects a perplexity that God himself shares.   Why do the people persist stubbornly in their false ways? Why do they choose to die?   Human nature is puzzling and irrational when contrasted with the behavior of animals and birds who are governed by an instinct for following Yahweh's ordinance (cf. Jer. 8:4–7).   The Book of Isaiah opens on a note of divine anguish.

> Sons [children] have I reared and brought up,
>> but they have rebelled against me.
> The ox knows its owner,
>> and the ass its master's crib;
> but Israel does not know,
>> my people does not understand [discern] (Isa. 1:2-3).

Here the parallel verbs "know" / "discern" refer to the trust, recognition, and faithfulness that characterize personal acknowledgement of God (cf. Ps. 46:10: "Be still and know . . ."). These poetic lines introduce Yahweh's controversy with the people (a "covenant lawsuit": 1:2-20) which includes the question as to why they continue to rebel even though the country is wounded from head to foot—doubtless a reference to the devastation wrought by Assyrian invasion (Isa. 1:4-9). Prophets like Isaiah surely would have argued that the words, "there is no health in us," belong essentially to a prayer of general confession!

One should not hastily conclude that the prophets assumed a "doctrine" of original sin as the basis for their proclamation. They were not interested in making generalizations ("all human beings are sinners"), and they did not even allude to the biblical story about Paradise Lost in Genesis 2—3. As pastoral theologians, they responded to the situations that they faced, whether in Ephraim or Judah. They saw all too clearly that the people were not living in a state of neutrality, with the freedom to turn one way or the other—toward the service of Yahweh or toward some other loyalty that promised meaning and fulfillment. Rather, the "heart" (mind, will) of the people was already committed, so that, like many modern people, they easily rationalized their behavior as morally and religiously acceptable. In turning to Baal, the god of sex and fertility, they believed that they were really serving Yahweh, the God of the exodus and Sinai. And in pursuing their "civil religion," with its nationalistic ambitions, they sincerely believed that they stood firmly in their own religious tradition. Later on, Jeremiah was to summarize the problem succinctly: "The heart is the most deceitful of all things, desperately sick; who can fathom it?" (Jer. 17:9, NEB).

Some critics attack religion from the outside, calling it the opiate of the people, regarding it as culture bound, condemning it as a projection of human wishes. The prophets, however, sympathetically criticized from within; for they had been brought up in the religious traditions of Israel and were profoundly influenced by cultic forms and language. They knew all too well that the deceitfulness of the human heart can become most subtle and pernicious in the sphere of our ultimate concerns, that is, religion and its corporate expression in worship. Ironically, religion can be an expression of apostasy or "sin," and the institutional forms of religion can be a manner of escaping from the one true God in order to serve an idol—a construction or projection of the imagination of the heart. This helps us to understand why the eighth century prophets were so fiercely critical of "organized religion": the services of worship, the temple, the cultic officials. Amos poked fun at the whole religious scene by giving a parody on a call to worship: "Come to Bethel and rebel, to Gilgal and sin boldly" (Amos 4:4a). The leaders of institutional religion (priests), according to Hosea, were parasites who "fed on the sin" of the people (Hos. 4:8). And Isaiah carried the criticism of services of worship to such an extreme that Yahweh would not even listen to prayer!

> When you spread forth your hands [in prayer],
>   I will hide my eyes from you;
> even though you make many prayers,
>   I will not listen;
> your hands are full of blood (Isa. 1:15).

Thus the human problem, as the prophets see it, is that the people are completely off course. Willfully they had turned from the allegiance which gave them identity, vocation, and future, and had turned to other loyalties or "faiths," which offered temporary benefits but in the long run would lead to disaster. Furthermore, they were so stuck in this false way of life that they did not even realize their predicament. Their religious outlook and their mode of worship only confirmed them in the pursuit of "the devices and desires of their own hearts," to use the language of a familiar prayer. What was the way out of the dilemma? When people are stubbornly committed to following their own self-defeating course, like stampeding horses plunging headlong into the thick of disaster (cf. Jer. 8:4–7), what power can arrest them and turn them around?

DIVINE INITIATIVE AND HUMAN RESPONSIBILITY

Here we find ourselves before one of the most baffling theological problems that arise out of the experience of the presence of God in the world. What is the relation between divine power and human freedom? It would seem that, to avoid utter contradiction, one would have to say either that God is in complete control, in which case human beings lose their responsibility, or alternatively, human beings are fully in control of their own destiny, in which case God is either severely limited or has absented himself from the world in order to leave things up to human beings. The surprising thing is that the prophetic message wants to hold on to both: God's unlimited power and human responsibility. God's presence does not take away human freedom but that very presence demands the exercise of responsibility; in fact, God's presence liberates people from bondage and gives them freedom in his service. Paradoxically, it is the servant who is free. George Matheson, the famous blind preacher (1842–1906), wrote a hymn that deals with this paradox of grace, the opening words of which are based on the prisoner theme of Ephesians 3:1:

> Make me a captive, Lord, and then I shall be free;
> Force me to render up my sword, and I shall conqueror be.

In treating the theme of repentance, the eighth century prophets begin, not with Israel's freedom to decide, but with the divine initiative which requires and grants freedom. Edmund Jacob, a French Old Testament theologian, properly observes: "The initiative of this return belongs to God himself."[6] The people are called to exercise their freedom and return to the covenant relationship; yet, paradoxically, it is Yahweh who moves the will to seek him through his own prior activity. The paradox is expressed beautifully in Hosea 14:1–8. The passage begins with an appeal to Israel to exercise responsibility and repent, with all that implies in the realm of politics ("Assyria shall not save us") and social relations ("In thee the orphan finds mercy"):

> Return, O Israel, to Yahweh your God;
>> for you have stumbled in your evil courses.
> Come with your words ready,
>> come back to Yahweh (Hos. 14:1–2a, NEB).

Yet behind this invitation to return is the divine initiative, manifest in the shocking and shaking crises of the time:

> I will heal their apostasy;
>> of my own bounty will I love them;
> for my anger is turned away from them (Hos. 14:4, NEB).

Thus the prophets proclaimed that God punctuated his people's history with crises that were intended as urgent calls for reorientation and redirection. God stood at every juncture of the way, so to speak, pleading for a return to the point where Israel moved in the wrong direction.

"PREPARE TO MEET YOUR GOD!"

This imperative is the subject of a poem in the Book of Amos which stands out as a separate pericope (4:4–13), though related to its present literary context. Notice the powerful movement of the passage. It begins with a tongue-in-cheek call to worship Yahweh at Bethel and Gilgal (4:4–5), northern sanctuaries hallowed by the aura of sacred tradition (Gen. 28:10–17; Josh. 3—4). "Come to Bethel and rebel. . . ." The main body of the poem (4:6–11) is the recitation of a series of earth-shaking crises, each one beginning with the announcement of what Yahweh did ("I sent," "I smote," "I overthrew") and each concluding with the solemn refrain, "Yet you did not return to me." The literary unit reaches its target point in verse 12 with the transitional "therefore," which introduces Yahweh's vow to do something final, though his act is unspecified:

> Therefore thus I will do to you, O Israel;
>> because I will do this to you,
>> prepare to meet your God, O Israel!

Appropriately the literary unit in its present form ends with a doxology (v. 13), which elevates thought beyond the level of idolatrous worship in Gilgal or Bethel to the transcendent majesty of Yahweh, who is Creator and Lord.

The intention of this poetry is homiletical: to awaken listeners to the meaning of the present by proclaiming the shock of God's future. It is improper to deduce the theological generalization that natural calamities such as famines, draughts, plagues, epidemics, earthquakes are "sent" by God. In a broad sense it is true that no event falls outside of the sphere of God's purpose; but one must be cautious about generalizing from this theological conviction to specific cases in the modern world and proclaiming that God sent a particular earthquake in Yugoslavia, a flood in Holland, an epidemic in Africa, or a famine in India. In this case, Amos was not speaking to the larger problem of natural evils that engulf all peoples but, specifically, to Israel's failure in her covenant responsibility. It is possible that he was drawing on a conventional list of "covenant curses" or plagues which were to be invoked in situations of covenant disobedience. In any case, Amos' homiletical intention was to remind the people that Yahweh had been at work in the crises of the past, punctuating their lives with urgent calls for repentance and seeking to bring them to a new awareness of their vocation as the people of God. Whatever had happened in the past, the people had been insensitive to the fact that God had met them at every turn of the road, trying to cure them of their blindness and pleading with them to return to the way that leads to life.

According to the prophets, Yahweh not only took the initiative to shock the people awake; he also placed before them the possibility of decision. It is striking that precisely in those homiletical contexts in which God's prevenient grace is stressed the emphasis falls heavily on a conditional *if*, as in the ancient Sinai tradition: "If you will obey my voice and keep my covenant . . ." (Exod. 19:5-6). We would expect this kind of preaching in the case of prophets like Hosea and Jeremiah who stood in the Mosaic covenant tradition. This tradition found homiletical expression in the conditionals of Deuteronomy, in terms of which the people were summoned to choose between life and death (Deut. 30:15-20). Hosea took the Sinaitic conditional covenant so seriously that he could even contemplate the possibility that Yahweh would terminate the covenant relationship. According to his prophecy the covenant formulation, "I am your God and you are my people," would be negated in the time of God's judgment: "You are not my people and I am not your God" (Hos. 1:9; cf. 1 Pet. 2:10). The same conditional accent is found, however, in the proclamation of the eighth century prophet, Isaiah of Jerusalem. Although this prophet stands primarily in the theological tradition of the unconditional Davidic covenant (2 Sam. 7) and does not refer at all to the exodus-Sinai tradition, he insists that faith in Yahweh, the King, involves conditional responsibilities. In the context of a covenant lawsuit against his people, we hear the appeal to argue a court case: "Come now, let us reason together, says Yahweh. . . ."

> If you are willing and obedient,
>   you shall eat the good of the land;
> But if you refuse and rebel,
>   you shall be devoured by the sword (Isa. 1:18–20a).

The sovereignty of God does not cancel out human obligation but, on the contrary, requires it and motivates it. The hard words given in connection with Isaiah's call (Isa. 6:9b–10; quoted in Matt. 13:10–15 and summarized in Mark 4:12; Luke 8:10) constitute no exception. Here we have a premonition that the prophet's mission will fail owing to the people's insensitivity, though the formulation "lest they. . . . [re]turn and be healed" implies that they could yet avert the threatened disaster and ruin by playing a responsible part.

This does not mean that repentance of the people would have transformed miraculously the political situation and averted Assyrian expansion. All four of the eighth century prophets were "prophets of doom." Unlike the popular prophets who filled the people's minds with vain hopes, promising that everything would be well (cf. Jer. 23:16–17), they announced that disaster was inevitable, given the internal corruption of the people of Ephraim and Judah and the external realities of the international world. The inevitable divine judgment, however, was not a fatalistic necessity, as in a Greek tragedy in which persons are caught in the clutches of the impersonal power of fate (moira) and bring upon themselves, willy-nilly, punishment (nemesis). Even though the present provides little grounds for optimism, the future is not closed, that is, predetermined to follow a plan that is programmed in advance. There is always the possibility that people will listen and turn from their evil ways, and there is always the possibility that Yahweh will be gracious. The word "perhaps" or "maybe" is theologically important in the prophetic message.

SEEKING THE LORD

The announcement that "perhaps Yahweh will be gracious" is found in a section of the Book of Amos (chap. 5) which in the Oxford Annotated Bible is put under the caption: "The horror and finality of Israel's deserved punishment." Right in the midst of a passage that portrays the gathering clouds of darkness and doom, we find the invitation—twice repeated—to "seek Yahweh [or "seek good"] and live!" (Amos 5:4–6 and 5:14–15).

Each of these little poetic units deserves close scrutiny. It is noteworthy that Amos uses a liturgical verb, "seek," which elsewhere refers to temple worship, where one may "seek Yahweh's face" or his presence (Pss. 24:6; 27:8). In the first poetic unit (5:4–6), Amos contrasts a genuine seeking of Yahweh with "seeking" famous sanctuaries hallowed by religious tradition: Bethel, Gilgal, Beersheba (southern prophets, like Micah, would have added Jerusalem to the list [e.g., Mic. 3:9–12; Jer. 7]). This passage emphasizes the negative side of the Divine Perhaps: "Seek Yahweh . . . lest he break out like fire. . . ."

In the corresponding poetic unit (5:14–15) the invitation is repeated, though with a subtle shift into the area of ethical responsibility: "Seek good, and not evil, that you may live." This should not be construed to mean that seeking Yahweh is the same as seeking the moral good, as though God were identical with the philosophical ideal of the Good or with the "social values" of the moral consciousness. As Wilhelm Vischer observes in a forceful sermon on Amos' theme of seeking Yahweh, the God of the covenant "turns upside down the scale of values" created by social class, so that "loved by God, we love what he loves and hate what displeases him."[7] Notice that the imperative "seek good, and not evil" is chiastically reversed in verse 15: "hate evil, and love good." This poetic unit, in contrast to the one previously considered, stresses the positive side of "the Divine Perhaps": Seek Yahweh, ". . . it may be that [he] will be gracious to the remnant of Joseph."

As in the case of other biblical passages that we have considered, it is not sufficient to consider these small poetic units by themselves, separated from their present literary context. The two invitations have a definite function in a larger poetic whole, which is important for interpretation. A careful study of the chapter would probably result in an outline something like this:

A. Yahweh's offer of life (5:1–9)
1. Lament on the imminence of death (5:1–3)
2. Yahweh's invitation ("Seek me," vv. 4–5), supplemented by the prophetic echo: ("Seek Yahweh," vv. 6–7)
3. Doxology (vv. 8–9)
B. Renewed offer of life (5:10–17)
1. Yahweh's indictment, followed by a consequence ("therefore"), twice repeated (5:10–11, 12–13).
2. The prophet renews the offer of divine grace (5:14–15)
3. The threat of death, evidenced in the death wail (*hôy*, "alas") in the cities and lamentation in the country (5:16–17), for Yahweh "will pass through the midst" of the people.

The poetry prepares for the announcement, introduced by *hôy* ("alas, woe"), that the Day of Yahweh will be darkness, not light (5:18–24). Yet in the midst of this macabre poetry, at two strategic points (5:4–6, 14–15), there is an offer of a new possibility, for "the God who threatens Israel with death can also give life."[8] Admittedly, in the proclamation of Amos the offer is restricted to the "remnant of Joseph" (5:15), a motif that is emphasized in Isaiah's message that, in the grace of God, there will be a remnant ("a remnant shall return"). No assurance is given that the people of God would survive in their present, visible form, owing to their involvement in social injustices and their precarious position in the path of powerful empires. Amos' message may sound harsh, but it strikes tones whose resonance is heard in the gospel of the New Testament: that in the midst of death God offers life, not as a guarantee of safety (Mic. 3:11b) but as the wonderful possibility—the "perhaps"—of his grace (cf. 2 Cor. 4:7–15).

WHEN GOD REPENTS

God's offer of life is accompanied by the threat of punishment: "lest he break out like fire in the house of Joseph, and it devour, with none to quench it for Bethel" (Amos 5:6). The preaching of the eighth century prophets is filled with oracles of judgment, in which the announcement is made that Yahweh will chastise his people.

> "For you alone have I cared
>   among all the nations of the world;
> therefore will I punish you
>   for all your iniquities" (Amos 3:2, NEB).

How are we to understand this punitive language?

In a chapter on "Chastisement" Abraham Heschel calls attention to the well-known legal distinction between punishment that is retributive (vindictive) and punishment that is deterrent (educative). He insists that "the divine intention, according to the prophets, is not primarily retributive, to impose penalty in consequence of wrongdoing; but rather deterrent, to discourage transgression by fear of punishment; and reformatory, to repair, to refine, to make pure by affliction."[9] Each prophet, of course, spoke with a different accent on the subject: Amos stressed the deterrent of God's punishment; Hosea believed that punishment could be reformatory as in a father's discipline of a child (Hos. 11); and Isaiah believed that punishment could have a cleansing power which, like fire, purges away the dross so that the pure remnant remains (Isa. 1:21–26). All of them employed the language of future punishment, not to stress an irrevocable decree, but to bring about in the present a confrontation with the faithful God who summons his people to decision and responsibility. The concern of prophetic preaching is to puncture the illusions of the people of God and to face them with the alternatives of life or death.

God's freedom in dealing with people is such that, as we hear in Mosaic tradition, he can "be gracious unto whom [he] will be gracious" and "show mercy on whom [he] will show mercy" (Exod. 33:19). Indeed, God himself may "repent," that is, modify his plan or course of action, either in response to a prophet's intercessory prayer (as in the case of Amos' first two visions, Amos 7:1–3, 4–6) or, even more important, in response to genuine repentance on the part of the people (see Jeremiah's parable of the potter and the clay, Jer. 18:1–11). The operative verb in these contexts is not *šûb* (repent) but *niḥam* (have a change of heart, relent).

The idea of God's repentance sounds strange to modern ears, and deserves clarification. Two things should be said. First, God's repentance does not mean that he is fickle or capricious, moved only by the whim of the moment. "The Glory [God] of Israel," we read in 1 Samuel 15:29, "will not lie or repent; for he is not a man that he should repent." The preaching of the prophets is based on the fundamental conviction of Israel's worship that God is faithful, trustworthy. Second, God's faithfulness is not rigid commitment to a prearranged plan or a decision announced in advance. Commenting on Jeremiah's parable of the potter and the clay, the Old Testament theologian Gerhard von Rad points out that there is an "immense freedom at God's disposal."[10] This freedom means that he reserves the right to amend or mitigate his judgment, subject to some change in the human situation.

Prophetic preaching is dominated by the awareness of the "immense freedom" which the God of Israel has in dealing with his people— a people forgetful of its roots, rebellious from the days of its youth, and determined to pursue the devices and desires of its own heart. The prophets sought to bring the people to realize that at the depth of the catastrophes which shook their lives and brought intense suffering, God was present, providing the impulse for the return from a road leading to ruin and offering a new life. The presence of God in the midst of his people prompted a later prophetic poet (Second Isaiah) to issue an invitation, one that is transposed into a new key in Christian worship:

> Seek Yahweh while he may be found [i.e., is present],
>   call upon him while he is near;
> let the wicked forsake his way,
>   and the unrighteous his thoughts,
> let him return to Yahweh that he may have mercy on him,
>   and to our God, for he will abundantly pardon (Isa. 55:6–7).

CHAPTER FOUR

WHAT THE LORD REQUIRES:
JUSTICE

A passage in the Book of Hosea (Hos. 11:12—12:14) provides a bridge that leads from the previous discussion of the theme of returning to God to the question that will engage us in this and following chapters: what does it mean to live rightly and acceptably before God? In this passage Hosea speaks to the contemporary situation in Ephraim by recalling traditions about Jacob, the ancestor and representative of northern Israel (Hos. 12:2–6). He recalls that Jacob was a wrestler, who struggled with his twin brother in the womb (Gen. 25:26) and who in his manhood strove with God (Gen. 32:22–30). But, above all, Jacob "met God at Bethel" (Hos. 12:4b), where he was assured that, with the help of Yahweh, he would return from exile in a foreign land (see Gen. 28:15, 21). The prophet then exhorts the contemporary children of Jacob to "return" (repent) in a deeper way:

> So you, by the help of your God, return,
>> hold fast to love (ḥesed) and justice (mišpāṭ),
>> and wait continually for your God (Hos. 12:6).

Two things are noteworthy about this verse. First, it is concerned primarily with "the *how* of her [Israel's] return . . . only the God of Israel can make this possible."[11] This recalls our discussion in the previous chapter. Second, the return is to be manifest in a new loyalty (ḥesed), the doing of justice, and an eager waiting for Yahweh, that is, a hope that strains toward the future. These are the characteristics of the life of a people whose existence is based on a faithful relationship to God.

It is striking that the terms of Hosea's exhortation correspond closely to Yahweh's threefold requirements summarized in the Book of Micah:

> God has told you what is good;
>   and what is it that Yahweh asks of you?
> Only to act justly, to love loyalty (*ḥesed*),
>   and to walk wisely before your God (Mic. 6:8, NEB).

This is one of the most "quotable quotes" in the Old Testament; the sentence was cited, for instance, in President Carter's inaugural address in January 1977. It is often regarded as the epitome of the message of the eighth century prophets, which included Amos' accent on justice (Amos 5:24), Hosea's emphasis on *ḥesed* or covenant loyalty (Hos. 6:6), and Isaiah's plea for the "humble walk" of faith (Isa. 7:9; 30:15). Actually, the three terms in Micah's summary should not be separated sharply from one another and assigned to particular prophets; not only do they overlap in meaning but also the same or equivalent terms are found in the preaching of all the eighth century prophets, for example, Hosea 12:6. Nevertheless, Micah 6:8 provides a good anchor point from which to consider what Yahweh requires of those who, to use the language of Christian liturgy, "truly and earnestly repent of [their] sins . . . and who intend to lead a new life, following the commandments of God and walking in his holy ways."

"O MY PEOPLE, REMEMBER!"

Let us consider the relation of Micah's summary to the larger literary context in which it is found (Mic. 6:1–16). It is not easy to trace the literary history of the chapter. Some maintain that Micah 6:1–8, which is usually regarded as a literary unity, is actually composed of two originally separate units: a) a law court dispute (*rîb*) found in verses 2–5; and b) a priestly teaching (*tôrāh*) given in verses 6–8. According to James Mays (*Micah*, p. 138), these two units were combined by an editor, who added verse 1 to integrate the material into a larger whole. Be that as it may, it is clear that the present form is that of a covenant lawsuit (*rîb*) in which Yahweh enters into controversy with his people (cf. Isa. 1:2–20 where sacrifices acceptable to God [cf. Rom. 12:1] are also evaluated).

The literary form reflects the setting of a court. In this judicial proceeding Yahweh is the plaintiff, and the prophet is his advocate or attorney. The literary pattern displays the following elements:

A. *Issue of a summons to a hearing* (vv. 1–2). As in the covenant lawsuit form elsewhere (Isa. 1:2–3; Jer. 2:5–13), the witnesses to the court proceeding are elements of God's creation: heavens and earth, mountains and hills. The court trial has a cosmic setting.

B. *Statement of the aggrieved party* (vv. 3–5). As in other covenant lawsuits (Hos. 4:1–3; Isa. 1:2–3; Jer. 2:5–13), Yahweh is the one who has been offended and he brings the charge: "O my people, what have I done to you . . . Answer me!"

C. *Statement of the aggrieving party* (vv. 6–7). The people, represented by the worshiper (the "I") who comes before God, raise the question of what sort of response is appropriate to Yahweh's overture. The question is carried to an impossible extreme for authentic Israelite faith: the sacrifice of the first-born as atonement for sin (cf. 2 Kings 23:10; Jer. 32:35).

D. *Response of the court* (v. 8). The only sacrifice acceptable to God (cf. Ps. 51:15–17) is a life that is characterized by justice, loyalty, and humility.

E. *The divine verdict* (vv. 9–16). As a result of Israel's covenant infidelity, legal sanctions ("curses of the covenant") will be invoked, including lack of nourishment, of family increase, and of fertility (cf. Mic. 6:13–15 with Deut. 28:15–19).

One of the key verbs in this covenant lawsuit is "remember": "O, my people remember . . ." (Mic. 6:5). In the syntax of the sentence, the verb (*zākar*) refers to the traditions of the conquest of Moab in East Jordan (Num. 22—24) and the march from Shittim in the Jordan Valley across the Jordan River to Gilgal (Josh. 3—4). The appeal to remember, however, also includes the exodus tradition mentioned in the preceding verse: "I brought you up from the land of Egypt, and redeemed you from the house of bondage . . ." (6:4). The Divine Plaintiff is shocked that Israel would forget the story that is the basis of her identity as a people and her knowledge of God (cf. Joshua's story recitation in Josh. 24:2–13). The purpose of remembering is to actualize the past, to make the story a present reality so that the people "may know the saving acts" (literally "the righteous deeds"; cf. Judg. 5:11; 1 Sam. 12:7) which display Yahweh's concern for his people and his relationship to them.

Another important verb in this context is found at the beginning of verse 8: "He has told you what is good. . . ." The verb (*higgîd*) refers to the announcement of the obligations ("laws") that are binding on those who have experienced God's liberating acts and who have been drawn into covenant relationship with him (cf. Joshua's promulgation of statutes and ordinances in the Shechem ceremony, Josh. 24:25–27). Torah includes both *haggadah* (story) and *halakah* (stipulations), or in our terms, gospel and law. Here "the good" does not refer to moral principles that are independent from God and which are grounded solely in moral consciousness. Rather, "the good," as we see from Micah 6:1–8, has been manifested in God's way with his people, and particularly his "righteous acts" on behalf of a weak and oppressed people. God's requirements—justice, loyalty, the humble walk—are given essentially within the story of his relationship with the Israelite people. If the people will remember that story, they will realize that Yahweh has shown them the kind of actions that befit the people of God. Recall that in Amos' message, "to seek Yahweh" (Amos 5:4, 6) is parallel to "seeking good" or "loving good" (Amos 5:14–15), that is, establishing justice.

THE UNIVERSAL AND THE PARTICULAR

In the prophecy of Amos, the theme of doing God's will ("the good") is set in the spacious context of international law, as evidenced by the oracles against the nations in 1:3—2:16 (see also the foreign oracles in Isa. 13—23). Except for the final section, where the prophet turns to Israel, all of the oracles have the same structure.

Introductory messenger formula: "Thus says Yahweh"
   A. Cause
      1. Announcement of inevitable divine judgment "For three . . . I will not turn it back"
      2. Reason: "Because they . . ."
   B. Effect
      1. God's act of judgment: "So I will send a fire . . ."
      2. Specific description of results
Concluding messenger formula: "says Yahweh"

In this manner the prophet announces that God's judgment will fall irrevocably on the surrounding nations for their various atrocities. Damascus (Syria) is excoriated for violence in the conquest of

Gilead (cf. 2 Kings 10:32–33). Gaza and Tyre are rebuked for slave traffic with Edom, a shameless betrayal of kinship ties ("the covenant of brotherhood"). Ammon committed terrible atrocities, including ripping up pregnant women, in connection with territorial expansion. And Moab is accused of the shocking indecency of burning to lime the bones of the Edomite head of state. And so it goes in the world of nations where power is an intoxicant that leads to excess. (The oracles against Edom in 1:11–12 and Judah in 2:4–5 may be later—though certainly appropriate—expansions of the prophetic announcement of divine judgment.) In each case, human actions and their consequences are understood as the cause and effect of God's judgment. However, Amos did not call the nations to accountability for the infraction of specific "laws," as though nations were bound together by international charter. He affirmed that Yahweh is the upholder of justice in the whole world, and it was from this standpoint of faith that he spoke out against violations of human rights in countries other than his own.

It is noteworthy that in this international context Amos blamed the people Israel more severely than other nations for their part in the crimes against humanity. He insisted that Yahweh, the God of Israel, is not a national god who protects and defends Israel's interests alone. To be sure, Yahweh brought the Israelites out of Egypt, but he was also at work in the histories of Israel's enemies, such as the Philistines who came from Caphtor (possibly Crete). He plays no favorites, and is impartial in his administration of justice.

> Are not you Israelites like Cushites to me?
>   says Yahweh.
> Did I not bring Israel up from Egypt,
>   the Philistines from Caphtor,
>   the Arameans from Kir?
> Behold, I, Yahweh God,
>   have my eyes on this sinful kingdom,
> and I will wipe it off the face of the earth (Amos 9:7–8a, NEB).

Amos' criticism of the doctrine of election, however, does not lead into a broad universalism, based on the "autonomous moral law" or the general moral consciousness. At the very climax of the proclamation to the nations, the prophet indicts Israel (2:6–8), then he asks the Israelites to remember the life-story that gave them existence, identity, and vocation as a people.   Notice the movement of thought in the passage 2:9–16:

A. "Yet I . . . " (2:9)
B. "But you . . ." (2:12)
C. "Hence"—the force of "behold" (2:13)

The "yet I" passage (introduced by the Hebrew adversative *waw*) is an appeal to remember the "saving acts of Yahweh" (cf. Mic. 6:5d): how he liberated his people from Egyptian bondage, led them during the wilderness sojourn, gave them a future in a new land, and raised up prophets to speak to them.   The "but you" sentence (again introduced by a Hebrew adversative *waw*) contains a brief rebuke to the people for their refusal to hear and understand. The "hence" section spells out the consequences of the people's failure.   In short, those who participate in the shared history of Israel should have a clear understanding of "the good," that is, what Yahweh requires, and hence they are called to greater accountability. "You only have I known . . .; therefore" (Amos 3:2).

YAHWEH LOOKS FOR JUSTICE

Referring again to the summary of God's requirements in Micah 6:8, let us consider the first demand upon the people of God: "to do justice."

The passion for social justice was shared by all of the eighth century prophets.   This theme was emphasized, for instance, by Micah, a citizen of a small village in the hills not far southwest of Jerusalem and a spokesman for the common people.   He regarded the leaders of the people as oppressors

> . . . who abhor justice,
>   and pervert all equity,
> who build Zion with blood
>   and Jerusalem with wrong (Mic. 3:9–10).

And in a prophecy later quoted at Jeremiah's trial (Jer. 26:18), Micah ventured to predict that, in the action-consequence sequence of Yahweh's justice, the future was bleak for Zion.

Therefore because of you
  Zion shall be plowed as a field;
Jerusalem shall become a heap of ruins,
  and the mountain of the house [temple] a wooded height
                                              (Mic. 3:12).

Isaiah, a man of the city and an adviser to the royal court, could not go so far as to predict the destruction of the temple which, according to his theological perspective, Yahweh had chosen as his "dwelling place" (Pss. 78:69; 132:13–18). Nevertheless, he was just as passionately concerned for social justice as Amos or Micah, as evidenced, for instance in his Song of the Vineyard (Isa. 5:1–7). This passage deserves special attention, for in both the Old Testament and the New the image of the fruitful/fruitless vineyard is one of the major metaphors for the people of God (Hos. 10:1; Jer. 2:21; Ezek. 19:10–14; cf. John 15).

Clearly the Song of the Vineyard is a separate literary unit—a pericope that can be snipped out of its present context without harm to its integrity. Such songs were sung, probably to the accompaniment of a stringed instrument, at the time of the Fall Festival (New Year's) when the people flocked to the Jerusalem temple to rejoice in the miracle of fertility that accompanied the rotation of the seasons. Isaiah borrowed the literary genre, with its theme of sexual fertility (cf. Song of Songs 1:41), for his homiletical purpose.

As used by Isaiah, the song proves to be not a song of joy but a lament, sung by the "friend of the bridegroom" (cf. John 3:29) who acted as the bridegroom's representative during a marriage festivity. Thus the poet begins by singing for his "friend" (*dôd*) a "love song" in regard to his vineyard. But who is the friend? And where is his vineyard? The first part of the poem invites a judgment from hearers about an ordinary vineyard that proved to be a failure in the production of grapes for wine. Subtly the poet shifts the accent to "my vineyard," hinting that he is not speaking literally but metaphorically. Moreover, hearers begin to wonder to whom the pronouns "I" and "my" refer: to a vinegrower? to the singer? or someone else? (vv. 3–4). Before this ambiguity is resolved, the decision is announced that the vinegrower (whoever the person "I" is) has decided to uproot the vineyard and convert the plot into a waste (vv. 5–6). Apparently, this is no ordinary person, for who could command the clouds that they pour no rain on it (v. 6b)? Only in the last line, introduced by the motive particle "for" (*kî*), does everything become clear. Yahweh is the One who planted the vine (cf. Ps. 80: 8–11); and the vineyard is his own people: "the house of Israel" and "the men [citizens] of Judah." Furthermore, the distinction earlier made between an expected harvest of good grapes and, instead, a shocking yield of "wild grapes" (v. 4), is explained finally in a word-play that cannot be rendered adequately in English. Of Yahweh, who planted, cultivated, and protected the vineyard, it is said (v. 7b):

> He looked for *mišpāt* [justice] but found *mispāḥ* [violence],
>   for righteousness [*ṣᵉdāqâ*] but found *ṣᵉ'āqâ* [plaintive cry for help].

Here, as in the case of other biblical passages that we have considered, it is important to consider the function of the literary unit in its context. The vineyard motif is anticipated, on one side, by Yahweh's controversy with leaders who have "devoured the vineyard" and taken the spoil of the poor (Isa. 3:13–15). Even the women, "the daughters of Zion," come in for their share of criticism (3:16—4:1). On the other side, the Vinegrower's decision to destroy the vineyard is followed by a series of death-wails ("woes") interspersed with the ominous "therefore" of divine judgment (5:8–30). It is possible that originally the Song of the Vineyard was followed by seven woes, the one in 10:1–4 coming between 5:23 and 5:24.

TO ACT JUSTLY

In the Song of the Vineyard Isaiah couples "justice" and "righteousness" in the poetic style known as synonymous parallelism, so called because the thought of the first line is repeated in the second. The same parallelism is found in Amos' ringing proclamation:

> Let justice roll on like a river,
>   and righteousness like an ever-flowing stream!
>   (Amos 5:24, NEB)

—where a contrast is drawn between a Palestinian wadi that dries up after the spring rains and a river that flows constantly. Justice and righteousness are combined in numerous other cases (e.g., Amos 5:7; Hos. 2:19; Isa. 1:21, 27; 9:7; Jer. 22:15), showing that, though they may not be strictly synonymous, their overlapping meanings can signify one divine requirement.

What is involved in acting justly or righteously? To understand the social message of the prophets we must banish from our minds a view that is deeply ingrained in Western culture, namely, that justice is behavior that conforms to an ethical or legal norm. Justice is done, we say, when a judge decides impartially in terms of legal norms and precedents; and people are righteous when they live up to standards accepted by their community, nation, or religious tradition. But the eighth century prophets use the terms "justice/righteousness" to refer to the fulfillment of responsibilities that arise out of particular relationships within the community—relationships between ruler and people, tribal heads and clanspeople, parents and children, citizens and resident aliens, priests and congregation, and so on. Each relationship has its specific obligation, and all relationships ultimately are bound by relationship to God. Admittedly, the prophets do not advocate "equality" in a radically modern sense, for in society not every person is equal in position, power, and responsibility. But every person, whether king or commoner, high or low in estate, old or young, has a God-given right, by virtue of membership in the covenant community, to a meaningful, fulfilling place in the fabric of social relationships. When the demands of various relationships are fulfilled, justice or righteousness prevails and there is *šālôm,* "peace" or "welfare." In short, ethical responsibility is not based on an abstract norm outside of, or above, the relationships of a community, but is motivated by the demands and blessings of life in community, within which persons are bound together in various relations and in relation with God.

In the light of this community-centered view of justice, it is understandable that prophetic criticism fell heavily on the leaders of the people: the rulers, landlords, priests, and judges. The eighth century prophets perceived that there was no "peace" (*šālôm*) precisely because power was used not to fulfill the demands of social relationships, but to oppress and to destroy life in community. The wealthy used economic power to grind the poor into the dust; rulers used their position, not to defend the fatherless and plead the case of the widow, but to enhance their own prestige; the courts were not functioning to obtain a rightful position for the weak and legally helpless; and the religious leaders used their influence to support the establishment and to silence any voice of conscience about the violence perpetrated in society.   Only of the exceptional ruler could it be said, as Jeremiah later said in the case of good King Josiah, that he did "justice and righteousness" (Jer. 22:15) by using his royal power to fulfill the demands of the relationship between king and people and to build up the community.

In their attack upon social injustice, the prophets were not concerned primarily about a psychological state, a feeling of being oppressed or inferior.   People may be oppressed without knowing it, or they may even prefer slavery ("the fleshpots of Egypt") to freedom.   The question of social justice is whether one actually has the power to take part in the relationships of society with dignity and responsibility.   Furthermore, the prophets did not advocate the notion that social reform comes about by first changing the "heart" of the individual and bringing about a one-to-one relation between a person and God.   They perceived that individuals live and move and have their being in a context of social relationships; therefore a "return to God" must be manifest in a change of the social conditions that crush the weak and helpless.

GOD'S ROLE AS JUDGE

At the heart of the traditions of the Old Testament is the announcement that Yahweh, the God of Israel and the Creator of the world, has a special concern for the poor and helpless—those who have no access to the means of power and whose condition is neglected or forgotten by those in power.   Victims of oppression cry out to Yahweh, the God who transcends all the power structures and idolatries of the world, in the confidence that his righteousness is a saving power that can restore an afflicted party to wholesome human relationships.   The Book of Psalms contains many laments in which oppressed people cry out for "justification," that is, for a restoration to their rightful place in the community.   When suppliants cry out in distress, "Judge me, Yahweh" (Pss. 7:8; 26:1; 35:24; 43:1), they appeal, not to the kind of judge who adjudicates accordings to "laws" or "norms," but to the Judge who takes action to obtain justice for those whose right is denied and whose life is unfulfilled.

The eighth century prophets expounded the theme of Yahweh's judging action with great force. As we have seen, they called Israel to remember the story of Yahweh's "righteous deeds" (Mic. 6:4–5; 1 Sam. 12:7)—the story which was basic to their existence and vocation as a people. Once they were slaves in Egypt, and in their distress they cried out to Yahweh, and he heard their voice and liberated them. What appalled the prophets was that former slaves had become enslavers of the poor; those who were once victims of oppression had become oppressors. Therefore, they proclaimed, Yahweh was on the verge of manifesting his righteous power in a new way, with the object of bringing into being a community of peace and welfare.

According to prophetic preaching, Yahweh's judging action has both a negative and positive aspect. Negatively, it overthrows oppressors and structures of oppression; positively, it vindicates the oppressed by restoring them to their rightful place in a community. Isaiah envisioned that the City, purified of dross in the fires of suffering, would represent the restored community.

> Zion shall be redeemed by justice,
>   and those in her who repent, by righteousness.
> But rebels and sinners shall be destroyed together,
>   and those who forsake Yahweh shall be consumed
>   (Isa. 1:27–28).

Thus divine judgment, which looms so large in the message of the eighth century prophets, is not the antithesis of salvation: it is part of the saving work of the God who, as Mary exclaimed in her psalm (The Magnificat), "has put down the mighty from their thrones, and exalted those of low degree" (Luke 1:46–55).

CHAPTER FIVE

WHAT THE LORD REQUIRES: COVENANT LOYALTY

The second term in the classical summary of the prophetic message found in Micah 6:8 is *hesed,* variously translated as "mercy," "[loving]kindness," "steadfast love," "loyal love," "constancy," "loyalty." Among the eighth century prophets, the term is found mainly in Hosea, who couples it with "righteousness" (10:12) or "justice" (12:6) to describe the lifestyle of those who return to God, that is, repent.

All of the terms of the linguistic trinity in Micah 6:8 are action words, as indicated by the verbal formulation: to *do* justice, to *love* loyalty, and to *walk* humbly with God. The prophetic summary refers to practice, not theory; to life as it is lived concretely, not to ideals or principles that belong in a realm of abstraction. This is evident in the conjunction of the word *hesed* with the infinitive form, "to love," a word-combination that made it advisable for RSV translators to depart from their usual practice of rendering the term as "steadfast love" ("to love steadfast love" sounds awkward) and to translate "to love kindness." The verb is significant. In prophetic usage "love," and its opposite "hate," mean the energetic devotion of one's whole being—will, thought, and feeling—toward or against an object, as when Amos says "hate evil, and love good" (Amos 5:15), or when Isaiah declares that Yahweh "hates" Israel's solemn assemblies (Isa. 1:13–14). Such passion, according to Micah 6:8, should characterize those who practice *hesed,* loyalty.

IMITATION OF GOD'S LOYALTY

At the beginning of this study it was pointed out that Jesus invited his hearers to go and learn what the word found in Hosea 6:6

means. (In Greek the Hebrew word under discussion is translated
eleos, "mercy" in Matt. 9:13.) Before turning to the crucial passage
in Hosea, however, let us consider the theological meaning of the
word *ḥesed* in a classical passage found in Exodus 34:6–7, a liturgical summary that is quoted a number of times in the Old Testament
(e.g., Ps. 103:8; Jer. 32:18; Jonah 4:2). The intention of the
liturgical summary in the context of the Sinai narrative is to disclose
the meaning of the name of Yahweh, that is, his *identity* in relation
to his people. The proclamation is:

> Yahweh, Yahweh, a God
> > compassionate and gracious,
> > long-suffering ["slow to anger"],
> > ever constant and true ["abounding in *ḥesed* and fidelity"],
> > maintaining constancy [*ḥesed*] to thousands,
> > forgiving iniquity, rebellion, and sin,
> > and not sweeping the guilty away . . . (Exod. 34:6–7, NEB).

This liturgical summary has an important function in the narrative
context of Exodus 32—34, which begins with the episode of the
worship of the golden calf and concludes with Yahweh's gracious
renewal of the covenant. The question is whether Yahweh can go
with and be with a people of this sort (Exod. 33:12–17), a people
so fickle that they turn away from the covenant while they are still
in the shadow of Mount Sinai! Yahweh's loyalty, on the other hand,
is steadfast, despite the people's weakness. He stands by his commitment faithfully, for he is rich in loyalty and fidelity, and continues or maintains his loyalty to "thousands of generations" (see
the translation of NAB). His constancy, however, is not "cheap
grace," for Israel's betrayal of the relationship will evoke divine
judgment, though on a limited, terminating basis: only to the third
and the fourth generation, that is, contemporary generations (parents,
children, grandchildren, great grandchildren). Yahweh's anger is
brief and does not cancel his steadfast love which continues unbroken through generations beyond number (cf. Isa. 54:7).

The use of the term *ḥesed* with respect to God's relationship to
his people must be understood in the context of political, social,
and interpersonal relations in ancient society, such as treaties,
marriages, or friendships. Studies of the term have shown that it

applies, not to relationships in which parties are strictly equal (peers), but rather to relationships in which one party is "superior" in the sense of having more power or influence by virtue of social position, though one's "position" may be altered by shifting circumstances. A good illustration is the friendship between David and Jonathan (1 Sam. 18—20), two men who were bound together in a "sacred covenant" (1 Sam. 20:8), literally, "a covenant of Yahweh." As long as Jonathan had the superior position (son of the king), it was his obligation as a friend to help David escape from Saul's pursuing wrath. But Jonathan made David promise that, when their roles were reversed and David rose to power, David would manifest loyalty (*hesed*) to him (1 Sam. 20:12-17). David's obligation of friendship lasted even beyond Jonathan's death, for he was determined to "practice *hesed*" to other members of Saul's family on account of Jonathan (2 Sam. 9:1, 3, 7).

Loyalty, then, is manifested by a stronger party toward a weaker party in the context of personal relationship. It is not a virtue or personality trait but rather it is something to be done, which accounts for the accompanying verbs "do," "maintain," "love" *hesed*. We must not think, however, of *noblesse oblige,* that is, people of high standing behaving nobly toward inferiors in a condescending manner, as when the rich give alms to the poor or members of the comfortable middle class send (income-tax deductible!) checks to various charities. Rather, loyalty arises from the relationship itself, not from any external law or social custom. It is an act of spontaneity and therefore of grace. Indeed, one is free to be loyal or not to be loyal, even though the weaker party in the relationship, in a time of distress, has no other source of help.

From this brief discussion it can be seen that the term *hesed* is peculiarly applicable to God's relationship to his people. His loyalty is based on his covenant commitment to them (Ps. 103:11, 17); when, in times of need, they appeal to him for help, he acts with spontaneous obligation, that is, grace (Ps. 33:18-22). In fact, when used theologically, the word refers primarily to God's faithfulness within the covenant relationship. In Hosea 6:6 (and Micah 6:8), however, the word applies to *the people's* reciprocal covenant obligation to God, obligation that also should be manifest in the faithful performance of responsibilities that strengthen and maintain the community. Yahweh has shown them "what is good" through his "saving acts" that demonstrate his spontaneous love and sensitive concern, but the people have failed to imitate his salutary actions. Like other prophets, Hosea addresses his criticism of Israel to those who have power—kings, landlords, and especially clergy, that is, those whose social position should enable them to help the weak and needy and to maintain a healthy, wholesome community.

A SPURIOUS RETURN TO RELIGION

The crucial text, Hosea 6:6, should not be read by itself, for it is an integral part of a larger literary unit that begins with 5:8 and extends perhaps through 7:16 (see H. W. Wolff, *Hosea,* pp. 103–130). The major theme that runs through this section is "returning to Yahweh" (repentance). The pericope shows that crisis may make a people more religious, but that there is a difference between a return to religion and a genuine return to God.

The structure of Hosea's proclamation to north Israel (Ephraim) may be outlined as follows:

A. *Cry of alarm* (5:8–15). Here the prophet acts both as a spokesman of God and a representative of the people. Urgently the prophet speaks about the shock of God's future, his intention being to call the people to "repent" before it is too late.

B. *Penitential song* (6:1–3). Perhaps this is quoted here as a priestly response on behalf of the people. The song, which clearly reflects popular Canaanite-style religion, expresses the superficial confidence that things are not so bad after all. Yahweh has hurt, but he will heal. "After two days . . . On the third . . .", that is, soon, he will resurrect the people from death on the analogy of the resurrection of the Canaanite god of fertility from the underworld.

C. *Divine oracle* (6:4–6). This is a response to the people's response, in which Yahweh expresses pained disappointment about his people's fickle loyalty.

D. *Divine judgment* (6:7—7:16). Here we find a depiction of Israel's false way of life—the powerful perpetrate violence, like robbers who pounce on the helpless, and this is condoned as a matter of government policy. Hence, a "harvest" is in store, that is, a historical catastrophe that will actualize the judgment of God.

Not always are we able to recapture the concrete life-situation into

which the prophetic word was spoken, but in this case it is evident
that the passage reflects the crisis of the Syro-Ephraimitic War (2
Kings 15:27–30; 16:1–20).   At this time, the Assyrians were on the
move, under the aggressive leadership of Tiglath-pileser III, hoping
to realize their dreams of world conquest.   In 733 B.C. two of the
kings whose territories lay in the path of conquest, Pekah of Ephraim
and Rezin of Syria, organized an anti-Assyrian coalition.   They attempted to force Judah to join the conspiracy, as we know from
Isaiah 7:1–17, but the effort was in vain.   Hosea 5:8–12 portrays
the devastation wrought in Ephraim, the northern kingdom.   The
Assyrian army swept down into the Jordan Valley, and from there
moved east into the plateau of Gilead and west into the hill-country
of Galilee.   Damascus, capital of Syria, fell in 732 B.C., and the
situation in Ephraim became desperate.   The anti-Assyrian king of
Ephraim, Pekah, was assassinated by a certain Hoshea son of Elah,
possibly with the help of Tiglath-pileser's undercover agents.   Hosea
5:13–14 reflects the ensuing crisis.   "When Ephraim saw his sickness," the next king, Menahem, switched loyalty to Assyria and
"went in haste to the Great King" (Hos. 5:13, NEB).   As we know
from Assyrian annals, "Menaham king of Samaria," along with other
peoples, pledged allegiance to Assyria by paying tribute.   To make
a long story short, it was a time of great political insecurity, as evidenced by Ephraim's diplomatic vacillation between Egypt and
Assyria (Hos. 7:8–9, 11) and the swift succession of rulers on the
throne of the northern kingdom (Hos. 7:3–7).   Not long afterward, when Assyria conquered Samaria (721 B.C.), the end came
for Israel. [See chronological chart, p. 4.]

Throughout this whole section, then, pulses the tension of a political and military crisis, enhanced by a feverish and vacillating foreign
policy (5:13; 7:8, 11) and a confused, if not chaotic, domestic
policy (5:11; 7:1–7).   The prophet was concerned with the inner
meaning of the crisis.   Would the crisis be the occasion for God's
therapy to work through the chastisement of suffering (cf. 7:1,
"When I would heal Israel . . .")?   Or would it only disclose that the
people's vitality was so sapped that premature senility ("gray hairs,"
7:9) had already set in and death was at hand?

The central part of this section, in which our key text (Hos. 6:6)
is found, opens with the voice of the Divine Lion (see 5:14) who
withdraws, taking his "prey" to his lair ("place"):

> I will return again to my place,
>> until they acknowledge their guilt
>>> and seek my face,
>> and in their distress they seek me (Hos. 5:15).

How does a people, especially the people of God, respond to the challenge of historical catastrophe?

The sharpness of this question in the original Hebrew text has been blunted by translations that interpret the connection between the final verse of chapter 5 and the opening verse of chapter 6 to be so close that in 6:1–3 Yahweh is still the speaker, who quotes (approvingly) the penitential words of the people. [Check your lectionary!] RSV, for instance, connects Yahweh's decision to withdraw "until they acknowledge their guilt" with the people's words in 6:1–3 by interposing the word "saying," though this connecting device (the equivalent of modern quotation marks) is definitely not in the Hebrew text. NAB suggests the same interpretation by punctuation (of course, not in the original Hebrew), namely, by placing a colon at the end of the last verse of chapter 5 and introducing the people's words at the beginning of chapter 6 with quotation marks. The Jerusalem Bible, on the other hand, appropriately makes a separation between the last verse of chapter 5 and the opening of chapter 6 and adds a new caption: "Israel's short-lived and shallow repentance." The commentator remarks that Hosea composed a penitential prayer that he put into the mouth of the people threatened by God's desertion and absence; in the crisis the people "exhort one another to return to Yahweh, verses 1–3, but the return is only temporary; there is no true repentance, verses 4–6." Similarly, NEB avoids establishing a connection between 5:15 and 6:1–3 which is not in the Hebrew. The people's words of penitence, according to this translation, are not quoted approvingly by Yahweh but are understood as "Israel's Apparent Remorse."

EVANESCENT LOYALTY

The roar of the Lion in the forest is followed by a passage (6:1–3) that seems to have its setting in the quiet of the temple. The people respond to the crisis with a penitential song, perhaps sung by priests on their behalf, which expresses their need to turn to God and their confidence that he is their refuge.

Come, let us return to Yahweh;
   for he has torn, that he may heal us;
   he has stricken, and he will bind us up.
After two days he will revive us;
   on the third day he will raise us up,
   that we may live before him.
Let us know, let us press on to know Yahweh;
   his going forth is sure as the dawn;
he will come to us as the showers,
   as the spring rains that water the earth (Hos. 6:1–3).

Notice the poetic contrast that is drawn between the "return" of the Lion to his lair and the "return" of the people. Even in the English translation some of the literary connections are apparent. For instance, the Lion says, "I will go, I will return . . ." (5:14, 15); the people sing, "Come [literally, "let us go"], let us return . . ." (6:1). The Lion threatens to "tear [his prey] and go off" (5:14); the people say, "he has torn but he will heal us" (6:1). [Author's translation]

This song is the prototype of many religious songs that have found their way into the liturgy and hymnody of the worshiping community through the centuries. Indeed, those with a sensitive ear will recognize that the notes of the song are echoed in religious songs today: the need to turn to God in time of trouble, sorrow about the sin that has brought divine affliction, assurance that God will not forsake his people, and the confidence that his salvation will come as gently as the dawn or the spring rains. Such songs may have their place, but Hosea quotes the people's song in this context to show that the people had a superficial view of the political crisis. In the first place, they believed that even though the seismic event was serious by any scale of measurement, it would pass quickly—after two or three days. Clearly they were under the influence of a popular, Canaanite-style religion which enabled them to take the judgment of God lightly. Though hard hit, the people had the resources for facing the situation triumphantly; indeed, they could have said, like later Judeans (or those who, more recently, have rebuilt modern war-devastated cities): "The bricks have fallen, but we will build with dressed stones . . ." (Isa. 9:10). And secondly, the people believed that they could count on divine help. Even though Yahweh had chastised them with suffering, he would not let them down.   After all, he had committed himself to the people in a covenant relationship, and therefore "on the third day" he would restore the normal state of affairs so that they could live in his presence.

The song is followed immediately by the central passage of this section (Hos. 6:4-6), in which Yahweh gives his exasperated response to the people's spurious return: "What shall I do with you . . .?"   Clearly, no real repentance has occurred; rather, Israel's loyalty (*hesed*) is as evanescent as morning mist ("cloud") or as the quickly evaporating dew (6:4).   Consequently, Yahweh has sent prophets, like Elijah and the eighth century prophets, to "lash"— indeed to "slay"—a fickle, disloyal, covenant-breaking people with his words (6:5).   One is reminded of the imagery of Jeremiah: Yahweh's word is like a consuming fire, or like a hammer that breaks rocks into pieces (Jer. 23:29-30).   What Yahweh desires is a covenantal loyalty, acted out in community relationships, that corresponds to his own faithfulness to his people.

> For I desire loyalty, not [animal] sacrifice,
> the knowledge of God, not whole burnt offerings (Hos. 6:6).
> [Author's translation]

Here the alternatives are stated sharply: not the sacrificial cultus but integrity and faithfulness in social relations; not the worship of God in elaborate ceremonies but sensing the claim of God in situations where the poor, the weak, and the oppressed cry for help!   It is clear, as many studies have shown, that the prophets were not against the forms of worship as such, but only against their corruption and misuse.   Nevertheless, we should not blunt the edge of the prophetic word by a facile "both-and" harmonization.   The prophets were not interested in balanced generalizations or with compromise between partisan interests.   Rather, their role was to "lash" and even "slay" the people with extreme, absolute words that call into question relationships to God and to fellow human beings.

THE KNOWLEDGE OF GOD

Hosea's statement about what Yahweh desires (Hos. 6:6) places in synonymous parallelism two terms: "loyalty" (*hesed*) and "the knowledge of God."   In their penitential song, quoted in 6:1-3, the people say: "Let us know, yes, let us strive to *know* Yahweh." The succeeding passage, however, which portrays Yahweh's exasperation (6:4–6), indicates that the people suffer from a defect in knowledge. Somehow this defect is related to their inconstancy, or lack of covenant loyalty. What does it mean to "know God"?

In the English language the verb "know" is ambiguous. The verb may refer to experiential knowledge (e.g., "I know Paul/Sally as a friend") or it may refer to the knowledge of abstract facts, in which area human beings are nowadays rivaled, or even excelled, by computers. Other modern languages are not burdened with this ambiguity. German, for instance, distinguishes between propositional knowledge (*wissen,* as in *Wissenschaft,* "science") and knowledge based on experience (*erkennen*). Similarly, the word "truth" is ambiguous. It may refer to factual accuracy: It is true that $2 + 2 = 4$; or it may refer to fidelity in personal relationships: She is a true friend, or There is no truth [integrity] in the land.

The Hebrew terms used by Hosea refer to the kind of "knowledge" or "truth" that is given in the context of personal experience and community relationships. This is evident from a little poetic unit in Hosea 4:1–3 with which the second section of the Book of Hosea (chaps. 4—14) opens. Here is another example of the literary form known as the covenant lawsuit (*rîb*), which we have considered previously in the case of Micah 6:1–8. The "controversy" initiated by Yahweh against his people displays a clear-cut structure.

A. Summons to the court hearing (4:1a)
B. Yahweh's accusation (4:1b–2)
C. Judicial verdict (introduced by "therefore"): the land and everything in it will languish (4:3)

This poetic unit is followed immediately by another (4:4–19) in which the accusation is laid specifically against the clergy (priests) for their failure to communicate "knowledge" (*da'at*) or *tôrāh* ("teaching"—"law" is not a fully adequate translation) to the people (4:6).

The terms of Yahweh's charge against Israel deserve special attention:

"There is no faithfulness or kindness [*ḥesed*],
    and no knowledge of God in the land (Hos. 4:1b).

The evidence for the accusation is given in various ruptures of covenant laws, including the Decalog: there is cursing (damning another person by misusing God's name; cf. Exod. 20:7; 21:17; 22:28), lying (deceitful cheating of one's neighbor in law courts or business; cf. Exod. 23:1-3, 6-9; Deut. 25:13-16), killing (premeditated murder; cf. Exod. 20:13; 21:12, 14; Deut. 27:24), stealing (Exod. 20:15), and committing adultery (Exod. 20:14). The list includes those crimes which mar or destroy relationships within the community, to the point that violence (literally "deeds of blood") is heaped upon violence (Hos. 4:2b).

It is clear from this covenant lawsuit that "the knowledge of God" is not a purely "vertical" dimension of faith, separated from the "horizontal" dimension of ethical responsibilities in the community. " 'Knowledge of God,' " as Hans Walter Wolff observes in this connection, "is not a second, different kind of 'religious' sphere in addition to the 'ethical,' as though one's relationship to God can be separated from his relationship with the neighbor. Rather, the phrase means knowledge of his teachings as the source of a harmonious community life within Israel."[12] These "teachings," as we have noticed in the covenant lawsuit in Micah 6:1-8, are mediated through the Israelite story in which Yahweh demonstrated by his own actions what is "good," that is, the meaning of covenantal "justice" and "loyalty." It is significant, then, that in the literary unit that follows Hosea's covenant lawsuit (4:4-14) the priests are "rejected" because they have "rejected knowledge" or, in other but equivalent terms, "have forgotten the *tôrāh* of your God" (4:6). The clergy, who know the tradition, are responsible for the plight of God's people: "My people are ruined for lack of knowledge" (4:6a). The function of priests is to preserve and communicate the tradition in which the people stand, so that the people may "know" (acknowledge) who God is and what his covenant demands and promises are. Failing in this, they hasten the day of a terrible famine—"not a famine of bread, nor a thirst for water, but of hearing the words of Yahweh" (Amos 8:11).

The covenant lawsuit just considered helps us to understand the statement in Hosea 6:6 in which "loyalty" (*ḥesed*) and "knowledge of God" stand in synonymous poetic parallelism. Both terms refer to the kind of personal relationship with God that is manifest in social responsibility—in actions that help to restore the poor and weak to meaningful and fulfilling relationships in the community and thus foster and maintain peace. It is in this ethical sense that Jeremiah, who had many affinities with Hosea, later spoke about the proper way to "know" God. At one point, he contrasted tyrannical King Jehoiakim with his father, good King Josiah (Jer. 22:13–16). Jehoiakim irresponsibly used his power to enlarge his palace and to live in fine style, but he lacked his father Josiah's "knowledge of God."

> Do you think you are a king
> because you compete in cedar?
> Did not your father eat and drink
> and do justice and righteousness?
> Then it was well with him.
> He judged [vindicated] the cause of the poor and needy;
> then it was well.
> Is not this to know me? says Yahweh   (Jer. 22:15–16).

The theme of "knowing God" is fundamental to Christian life and witness. In the Johannine writings, for instance, we find the teaching that "he who does not love does not know God; for God is love" (1 John 4:8). In the Christian community, "knowing God" often has been interpreted to mean knowing (loving) God in a mystical sense, or this "knowledge" has been restricted to the area of family relationships, or giving alms (charitable gifts) to the poor, or rescuing perishing victims of society and bringing them into the spiritual haven of the church. However, when the Christian gospel is heard in the wider context of the proclamation of Israel's prophets, this "knowledge of God" finds expression in social action that alleviates the distress of the oppressed and seeks to overcome the powers and conditions that create oppression and destroy life in community. It was Jesus himself who asked the "righteous," a constituency that is much larger than the original audience, to go and learn what the prophetic word in Hosea 6:6 really means.

CHAPTER SIX

WHAT THE LORD REQUIRES:
THE HUMBLE WALK

The final term in the ascending series found in Micah 6:8 is "to walk humbly with your God," or as the New English Bible translates, "to walk wisely with your God." The modifier translated "humbly/ wisely" is based on a rather unusual Hebrew root that occurs elsewhere only in wisdom literature, where it suggests the modest, restrained, cautious attitude befitting a sage. Thus we read in Proverbs 11:2:

> When pride comes, then comes disgrace;
> but with the humble is wisdom.

More and more we are coming to realize that the prophets, beginning with Amos, were profoundly influenced by Israel's wisdom movement which had its source in the period of Solomon, or even earlier. To be sure, they were often critical of the wisdom of the wise; they were against the kind of wisdom that inflates people with conceit and presumption (cf. Jer. 8:8–9.) But they had no hesitance in using the language and literary forms of the sages, as we noticed when considering the disputation in Amos 3:3–8. Above all, prophets heartily agreed with Israel's sages that the basis of true wisdom is reverent humility before God, the posture advocated in a key wisdom text: "The fear [reverence] of Yahweh is the beginning of wisdom" (Prov. 9:10; Job 28:28; Ps. 111:10, etc.).

"TO HUMBLE THE PRIDE OF ALL GLORY"

Micah's exhortation to walk humbly with God echoes the fundamental tone in the message of Isaiah of Jerusalem, whose ministry covered most of the last half of the eighth century B.C. (ca. 742–700

B.C.). During that tumultuous period, when Assyria was revising the political map of the world, Isaiah proclaimed that Yahweh, the Holy One of Israel, is King absolutely—cosmic King and sovereign over the nations—and that he comes majestically "to humble the pride of all glory, to dishonor all the honored of the earth" (Isa. 23:9). Before Yahweh's transcendent majesty, no human power can claim to be sovereign, no historical institution can presume to be absolute, no cultural value can boast ultimacy.

According to Isaiah's account in Isaiah 6:1–13, the vision of Yahweh's exaltation and the human response of humility and penitence were the major elements of his experience in the temple, which thrust him into society as a prophet.

> Woe is me! I am lost,
> for I am a man of unclean lips
> and I dwell among a people of unclean lips;
> yet with these eyes I have seen the King,
>   Yahweh of Hosts (Isa. 6:5, NEB).

Isaiah's experience was influenced by his upbringing in proximity to the Jersualem temple and especially by the Davidic theological tradition in which he stood. Other eighth century prophets, as we have seen, understood their mission and proclaimed their message in the context of a "story" or tradition that reached back to the exodus from Egypt. This was clearly the case with Hosea, who was profoundly influenced by Israel's sacred history (Hos. 2:14–15; 11:1; 13:4). Amos, too, appealed to remembrance of the story (Amos 2:9–11), and the challenge to remember is a basic element in the covenant lawsuit in Micah 6:1–8 (see also Jer. 2:4–13). But strikingly, Isaiah of Jerusalem (whom we distinguish from "Second Isaiah," a disciple of the prophet whose poetry is found in Isa. 40–55) does not appeal to the Mosaic tradition at all. His preaching soars above the so-called *Heilsgeschichte*—that is, the history of God's saving work evident in the exodus, sojourn in the wilderness, and entrance into the land—and concentrates on Yahweh's transhistorical, eternal rule.

In Isaiah's theological perspective, Yahweh's eternal rule (or kingdom) is manifest on earth through two "sacral" institutions: kingship and temple. The first of these institutions is alluded to obliquely in the opening words of Isaiah's account (Isa. 6:1), where he says that in the year that King Uzziah died he saw Yahweh seated on his throne, "high and exalted," in transcendent majesty. The reference to Uzziah's death (742 B.C.) signifies more than a dating of Isaiah's vision. Uzziah was a Davidic king whose reign, like that of all kings in the line of David, represented Yahweh's rule on earth. One basic tenet of royal covenant theology was that Yahweh made an "everlasting covenant" or covenant in perpetuity with David, assuring him of the continuity of his line and promising blessing for his kingdom (2 Sam. 7; Pss. 89, 132) which would even spill over into the lives of other peoples (Ps. 72:17; cf. Gen. 12:1-3). The Davidic king ruled on the throne of Jerusalem as the Son of God (2 Sam. 7:14a; Ps. 89:26; cf. Ps. 2:7), that is, Yahweh's elected representative on earth!

The second saving institution is the Jerusalem temple, the setting in which Isaiah received his inaugural vision. Another basic tenet of royal covenant theology was that Yahweh had chosen the Jerusalem temple as the place of his sacramental presence in the midst of his people (Pss. 78:67-72; 132:13-18). It was in the temple that Yahweh was enthroned in the Holy of Holies above the ark, his throne-seat, flanked on either side by cherubim (Exod. 25:16-22; Ezek. 10:1-5). According to psalms that celebrate Yahweh's kingship (Pss. 47, 93, 96—99), it was in the temple that the cultic exclamation was raised, "Yahweh is King!" One of the hymns of Yahweh's enthronement begins:

> Yahweh is king!
>   the peoples are perturbed;
> he is throned on the cherubim!
>   earth quivers (Ps. 99:1, NEB).

In Isaiah's vision the earthly temple fades into Yahweh's heavenly temple, where the prophet finds himself in the presence of the cosmic King who speaks before his heavenly council and summons a messenger to speak for him to the people of Jerusalem. Undoubtedly poetic imagination was influenced by the ancient mythical view of the correspondence between the heavenly temple and its earthly replica, the macrocosm and the microcosm (Exod. 25:9; cf. Heb. 8:1-7). According to this theological perspective, which was influenced by ancient Near Eastern views of kingship and temple, Yahweh's rule as cosmic King in his cosmic temple is manifest sacramentally through the reign of the Davidic king (God's "son") and in the Jerusalem temple worship (God's "dwelling place" or tabernacle). Isaiah's message moves in the dimension of Yahweh's eternal kingship that transcends Israel's sacred history and the histories of all peoples. Yahweh is "the Holy One of Israel"—a favorite expression of Isaiah (1:4; 5:19, 24; 10:20), but his glory fills the whole earth.

THE ARROGANCE OF POWER

The appropriate response to Yahweh's utter holiness—the theme of a heavenly anthem with its "Holy, Holy, Holy" (Isa. 6:3)—is humility and penitence. So it was in Isaiah's temple experience: he confessed his unworthiness and inadequacy and yet came to know the cleansing, renewing power of divine forgiveness (Isa. 6:4–7). Isaiah's task, however, was not to minister to the inner anxieties and guilt-feelings of individuals in isolation from the problems of society. The vision of Yahweh's exaltation above everything human and historical sharpened his awareness that he, as an individual, lived in the midst of a people of "unclean lips" (i.e., also unworthy and unfit to stand before the holy God). The message Isaiah was commissioned to speak to "this people" was so severe that it would be heard but not understood, until an arrogant people, enslaved by its own style of life and thought, had experienced the ominous judgment of God (Isa. 6:8–13).

In this situation Isaiah, more than any other eighth century prophet, perceived the arrogance of power—power which corrupts and which, when carried to its fulfillment, attempts to usurp the sovereignty of God. As we have seen earlier (Chapter Three), he denounced the "arrogant boasting" and "haughty pride" of the Assyrian dictator (Isa. 10:12), who supposed that his power was absolute and that he controlled the course of history. Isaiah's vision of divine transcendence prompted him to denounce all trust in military power and in the state which deifies military might (cf. Hab. 1:11: "whose own might is their god"). Nor did the arrogance of political and economic power escape his criticism. In the present arrangement of Isaiah's prophecy the death-wail (*hôy*, "woe," "alas") against Assyria in Isaiah 10:5–19 is preceded by another wail ("woe") against those who use the courts of law to dispossess the poor of their rights in society (10:1–4):

> Woe to those who decree iniquitous decrees,
>   and the writers who keep writing oppression,
> to turn aside the needy from justice,
>   and to rob the poor of my people of their right,
> that widows may be their spoil,
>   and that they make the fatherless their prey! (Isa. 10:1–2)

At one point in his book on *The Prophets*, Abraham Heschel reflects on the historical dilemma of unchecked, arrogant power: "Why are so few voices raised in the ancient world," he asks, "in protest against the ruthlessness of man? Why are human beings so obsequious, ready to kill and ready to die at the call of kings and chieftains?" He goes on to suggest that perhaps this is because people, then and now, are dazzled by "the splendor and the pride of kings," and unaware of the fact that "inherent in power is the tendency to breed conceit."[13] The deceitful, presumptuous impulse to be "like God" (cf. Gen. 3:5) is the theme of a taunt-song found in Isaiah 14:3–23. Though it comes from a period later than Isaiah of Jerusalem, when Assyria was superseded by Babylonia, it is consonant with a fundamental concern of the prophet. In the case of the Babylonian tyrant also, power bred conceit:

> You said in your heart,
>   "I will ascend to heaven;
>   above the stars of God
> I will set my throne on high;
> I will sit on the mount of assembly
>   in the far north;
> I will ascend above the heights
>   of the clouds,
> I will make myself like the Most High."
> But you are brought down to Sheol,
>   to the depths of the Pit (Isa. 14:13–15).

For Isaiah, as for Paul later (1 Cor. 1:25–31), the question is:

What do human beings actually have to boast about? Humanly speaking, there seem to be ample grounds for boasting: imperial pride and renown, military strength, urban prosperity, commercial success. Isaiah, however, sounds a note that is also heard in Psalm 20:7:

> Some boast of chariots, and some of horses;
>   but we boast in the name of Yahweh our God.

He takes away any ground for human boasting by lifting our minds to the transcendent sovereignty of God who judges all human conceits and thereby relativizes all human values and aspirations. Absolute power, according to Isaiah's message, is vested in God alone. Everything in the world, whether emperors and kings, chariots and fortifications, or the idols made by human hands (Isa. 2:8), are divested of their false claims of sovereignty.

IN JUSTICE YAHWEH IS EXALTED

In popular expectation, as we have seen earlier, the Day of Yahweh was to be a time when Yahweh would vindicate (get justice for) his people Israel by elevating them to a position of prestige among the nations and by downgrading or punishing their enemies. Agreeing essentially with Amos (Amos 5:18–20), Isaiah proclaimed that the imminent Day would be the Day of Yahweh's elevation in righteousness, the corollary of which would be the humbling of all peoples, including Israel, before his divine majesty.

Isaiah's poem on the Day of Yahweh in Isaiah 2:6–21, whose cadences are punctuated with recurring refrains concerning the elevation of Yahweh as King, is a powerful expression of prophetic vision. The poem apparently falls into three parts.

A. Verses 6–11. The poem opens with the ominous note that Yahweh has abandoned his own people, the reason being given in a series of sentences which open with the same verb ("to be filled with"). Their land is

> filled with foreigners who ply their trades
> filled with limitless silver and gold
> filled with limitless military equipment
> filled with man-made idols that claim devotion.

These tokens of Israel's glory will be worthless on the Day when people encounter the holy presence of Yahweh, the King. As though a world-wide holocaust were at hand, people were urged to flee to the caves and holes in the ground for protection. The stanza reaches a climax with the refrain (v. 11):

> Humanity's proud eyes shall be humbled,
>> people's pride shall be abased,
> And Yahweh alone shall be exalted on that Day.
>> [Author's translation]

B. Verses 12–17. The last word ("Day") of the previous stanza is picked up at the beginning of the next stanza: "For Yahweh of hosts has a Day. . . ." Moving from the realm of nature to that of history, the poet forcefully portrays the impact of Yahweh's Day in a series of sentences, each of which begins with the same Hebrew words (*'al kôl*). Yahweh's Day is "against all that is proud and lofty":

> against all the tall cedars of Lebanon and the lofty oaks of
>> Bashan
> against all high mountains and lofty hills
> against every high tower and fortified wall
> against all the proud ships that ply the waters.

Once again the stanza reaches a climax in the announcement that humankind will be humbled and "Yahweh alone will be exalted on that Day" (2:17; cf. v. 11).

C. Verses 18–21. It is not clear where the third poetic cadence begins, but apparently the poet picks up tones struck earlier, namely, the folly of idolatry (v. 8) and the flight to the caves (v. 10). Twice it is stated that idols will be useless (vv. 18, 20), and that people will flee for refuge (vv. 19, 21)

> from before the dread of Yahweh,
>> and from the splendor of his majesty,
> when he rises to terrify the earth.

The ensuing verse 22, which advises us not to place any confidence in mortal man in whose nostrils is breath (cf. Gen. 2:7), is lacking in the Greek translation (Septuagint) and seems to be a later comment from an Israelite sage (cf. Ps. 104:29). The verse, however, is another reminder of the affinity of the prophetic warning against human pride to similar advice in wisdom teaching. In both cases, humble faith calls into question all human values and achievements and permits nothing to parade as final or absolute.

Isaiah's poem gives powerful expression to the prophetic proclamation that Yahweh is King absolutely and that, in his holy presence, all human values and cultural pride are ultimately bankrupt. One key text, however, adds a further dimension to his poem on the Day of Yahweh. Indeed, the suggestion has been made that at one point in the poem (after 2:9) we should insert these words found in Isaiah 5:15–16:

> Humanity is brought low, humankind is abased;
> > haughty eyes are humbled.
> But Yahweh of hosts is exalted in justice,
> > the Holy God proves himself holy by righteousness.

There is no textual basis for transposing these verses, but they help us to understand the theme of "the dread of Yahweh" in the poem (2:10, 21). The encounter with the Holy God on his Day will be dreadful only because, in contrast to the proud and the mighty on earth, he demands and executes justice. Here Isaiah gives his own exposition of a major theme of Israel's psalms, one that celebrates Yahweh's coming to inaugurate his kingdom on earth as it is in heaven. All of nature is summoned to sing for joy, before Yahweh, who comes "to judge the earth" (Ps. 96:11–13)

> He will judge the world with righteousness,
> > and the peoples with his truth (Ps. 96:13b).

Thus for Isaiah, as for the other prophets, the experience of the holy is not an encounter with mysterious, numinous power, wholly beyond the mundane sphere where human beings struggle to find meaning and fulfillment in society. He stands firmly in the Mosaic tradition which testified to the in-breaking of divine holiness into the world with redemptive concern and ethical demand.

> Yahweh secures justice
> > and the rights of all the oppressed.
> He made known his ways to Moses,
> > and his deeds to the children of Israel (Ps. 103:6–7, NAB).

The holiness of Yahweh, then, is manifest as saving power directed toward the realization of justice/righteousness. Therefore, those who "boast" should boast that they "know" (acknowledge) Yahweh who "executes righteousness and justice in the earth" (Jer. 9:23–24).

LIVING UNDER TENSION

Isaiah's proclamation of the kingship of Yahweh was a summons to responsibility—to walk humbly with God—rather than a paralyzing surrender to historical inevitability or fate. Throughout his ministry he was an adviser to kings who had to cope with major political crises: the Syro-Ephraimitic War (735–732 B.C.), the fall of Samaria, capital of the northern kingdom (722–721 B.C.), the Assyrian siege of Ashdod (712–711 B.C.), Sennacherib's invasion of Judah (701 B.C.). He maintained that the fundamental basis for detente, that is, relaxation or easing of political tensions, was faith in God's overruling purpose. [See chronological chart, p. 4.]

A first-hand witness to Isaiah's message during the Syro-Ephraimitic crisis is given in the prophetic report in prose (7:1—8:15) which, in the present arrangement of the Book of Isaiah, is connected immediately with the report of Isaiah's call (chap. 6). A few years after Isaiah's public ministry began, encircling forces of small nations—Ephraim and Syria to the north (2 Kings 16:5–9) and Edom and Philistia to the south (2 Chron. 28:17–18)—attempted to force the kingdom of Judah into an anti-Assyrian coalition. As we have seen, Hosea faced the same crisis within Judah's sister kingdom Ephraim and he proclaimed that Ephraim's defect was lack of loyalty (*hesed*) and knowledge of God (Hos. 5:8—6:6). The southern prophet Isaiah, however, responded to the crisis from a different standpoint. The allies threatened to depose the Davidic king, Ahaz or Jehoahaz, and to put in his place a non-Davidic puppet who would play their political game (Isa. 7:6). Remember that Isaiah shared the convictions of royal covenant theology: Yahweh's kingship on earth was manifest through his elected Davidic king and through his elected sanctuary of Zion.

Isaiah's encounter with King Ahaz, related in Isaiah 7:1–17, is a dramatic one. Having his little son Shear-yashub ("A Remnant Shall Return") by the hand, Isaiah met King Ahaz at a critical moment, when he was inspecting the water supply of the city. They met in the vicinity of the Upper Pool near the Virgin's Spring (Spring of Gihon) on the eastern border of the city, from which a gently sloping aqueduct ("the waters of Shiloah," 8:6) carried water outside the city walls around the curve of the hill of Ophel southward to a Lower Pool. The spring supplied the city with water, especially precious in a time of military siege, and enabled the irrigation of land in the Kidron Valley.

The passage falls into two parts: a) the prophetic word (7:1–9) and b) the prophetic sign (7:10–17). Christian readers are apt to concentrate on the second part (the sign), raising such questions as: Who is this wonder-child? Who is his mother? What is the manner of the child's birth? Under what circumstances would he be born and grow up? How did the Hebrew word 'almāh, which refers only to a young woman of marriagable age, come to be taken as a prophecy of the Virgin Birth (Matt. 1:23; cf. Luke 1:27)? These questions have their proper place. It is important, however, to concentrate on the *relationship* between the two parts of the account: prophetic word and prophetic sign. In the Old Testament a futuristic sign, introduced by the formula "this shall be a sign unto you," is given to confirm a word of God already spoken. The word precedes the sign; the sign confirms the word by giving it visibility and actuality—to those who perceive in faith. Even when they spoke in the future tense, the prophets were concerned primarily about the urgency of the present. Accordingly, we shall concentrate on the prophetic word concerning faith, postponing to a later chapter consideration of future (messianic) hope.

The prophetic word was spoken into a situation of great tension and anxiety. "The heart of the king and the people," so we read, "trembled as the trees of the forest tremble in the wind." The pusillanimous king of Judah, Ahaz, was no match for the crisis. His throne was at stake, for the allies wanted to get rid of him. Moreover, the crisis had a spiritual dimension: would God go back on his unconditional promises of grace to a Davidic king (cf. the lament in Ps. 89:38–51)? The king, suffering a failure of nerve, was thinking of sending to Assyria for help, though at the expense of making Judah a vassal state of the empire.

Isaiah, however, saw the political crisis in the larger perspective of faith in the God who sits enthroned as eternal King, before whom all the events of human history take place (cf. Ps. 33:13–17). Indeed, the prophet addressed the king in language that reflects the ideology of Holy War, with the pre-battle "oracle of salvation." As in instances found elsewhere in Israelite tradition, the oracle began with the admonition to "fear not" (Isa. 7:4; cf. Exod. 14:13; Josh. 1:9) and to have faith in Yahweh of hosts who fights his battles in his own way. In this perspective, it was foolish to fear small nations like Syria and Ephraim, whose power was already exhausted, like a burnt-out torch. The "oracle of salvation" reaches a climax in verse 9b. The Hebrew words cannot be adequately translated into English:

'im lō' ta'ᵃmînû	If your faith is not firm,
kî lō' tē'āmēnû	you will not stand firm.

This may be paraphrased: "If your faith in Yahweh the King is not sure, your Davidic throne will not be secure." Abandon human alliance and put your affiance in Yahweh, for no conspiracy of nations can prevail against Yahweh who has chosen the Davidic king to be his son and Zion to be his holy hill (Ps. 2). Isaiah's call for humble faith is akin to the great psalm concerning the City of God, which reaches a climax in the oracle addressed to the tumultuous nations: "Let be then: Learn that I am God, high over the nations, high above the earth" (Ps. 46:10, NEB).

Isaiah's counsel to relax ("let be") and walk humbly with God has two dimensions, the one pragmatic and the other theological. At the level of pragmatic politics, the prophet offered the king a helping hand by trying to prevent him from engaging in a suicidal foreign policy. He urged the king to avoid panic and take a realistic view, for the attacking kings were weak incumbents who had almost exhausted their resources. There are times in politics, to echo the words of an American president, when "the only thing to fear is fear itself." Isaiah's word was not a call to political inaction but to a cool-headed realism in the face of the immediate emergency.

Isaiah, however, was more than a pragmatic politician, for his oracle of salvation was based on his vision of divine transcendence. Despite their pretensions and anxieties, human beings do not carry the burden of the world, Atlas-like, on their frail shoulders. The kingdom belongs to God, and he is free to open up unexpected possibilities, even though people find themselves in what seems to be a no-exit situation. Faith in God, then, liberates people from misplaced faith in human efforts to plan, shape, and control the future.

THE WATERS THAT FLOW GENTLY

Isaiah's call for a tranquil and humble walk with God proved to be too heavy a demand, except perhaps for a remnant of disciples who gathered around the prophet (Isa. 8:11–22). His theme of humble faith is expressed exquisitely in a passage that has come to be a favorite for many.

> In returning and resting you shall be saved;
> In quietness and trust shall be your strength (Isa. 30:15).

The basis of security, said the prophet, lies in a "return to God" and quiet, relaxed confidence in his sovereignty. Usually readers ignore the sequel to this oracle, in which the people respond by saying that they will have none of it and express their determination to place their confidence in speedy horses, that is, the best military defense. The attitude of King Ahaz was not different. Isaiah had supplemented his word—his oracle of salvation—with the promise of a confirming sign: the birth of the Immanuel child. Difficult times lay ahead, according to the prophecy, but before the child reached the age of discretion when he knew the difference between right and wrong, the frightening coalition of kings would be dissolved and the crisis would be over (Isa. 7:10–17). Ahaz, however, lacked the faith to hear the prophet's word or to wait for the confirming sign and, taking a desperate political risk, cast his lot with Assyria. After all, he had to be "practical" in facing the political realities of the moment. According to 2 Kings 16, he appealed to Tiglath-pileser to come to his rescue and even emptied the temple and palace treasuries to court his favor.

It is important to read the account in Isaiah 7:1–17 in its present literary context. On the one side, we find the report of Isaiah's vision of, and commission by, the transcendent King and the gloomy foreboding that the prophet's message would have no effect in prompting the people to return to Yahweh (Isa. 6). On the other side, we find prophetic words of threat (7:18–25) and ominous judgment (8:1–10). The imagery in 8:5–10 makes a great poetic impact. Because "this people" have spurned "the waters of Shiloah that flow gently," and have put their confidence in the might of Assyria, Yahweh will bring upon them a devastating flood from the Euphrates. The figure of speech harks back to the scene reflected in Isaiah 7:3, where Ahaz went out to inspect the city's water supply, including Shiloah, a canal from a life-giving spring. The Shiloah waters flowed in a small and quiet stream, yet they were the source of vitality for the gardens of the Kidron Valley and for the city itself. Therefore they symbolized the power of God's invisible rule that is bestowed silently and gently on his people. The mighty Euphrates River, by contrast, fed many "channels" or irrigation ditches; in the spring, when the snow melted in the high mountains to the north, it swelled into potentially destructive streams that overflowed all its banks and flooded the land (8:7).

Thus the prophet put before king and people a question that is both realistic and radical. What is the basis of ultimate trust? Do people look to the gently flowing waters of Shiloah, representing the silent and invisible power of God's kingdom? Or do they turn to the mighty waters of the Euphrates, representing the imposing pride and power of empire? Isaiah calls for a faith that transfers commitment from what is human and transient to what is absolute and eternal: the transcendent God, Yahweh the cosmic King. Those who walk humbly with God, the prophet declares, can face the crises of life unafraid and can live toward God's future "in quietness and trust."

CHAPTER SEVEN

GOD WHO CARES

In the last three chapters we have considered what God requires of his people, following the ascending summary given in Micah 6:8. The court-room setting of that passage might lead one to suppose that the relationship between God and people is "legal": God is a Judge (in the modern sense of the word) who makes legal demands on his people and issues a sentence of judgment for their failure to live up to the requirements of the law. According to this view, there is a contrast between the God of justice (law) and the God of mercy (love). Indeed, some people, unwitting disciples of the second-century heretic Marcion, maintain that the relationship between the Old and New Testaments is one of contrast: the God of Moses and the prophets is the God of justice and wrath, the Father known through Jesus Christ is the God of love and reconciliation. Viewed in this perspective, the Old Testament has been superseded by the Christian gospel. The role of the prophets is to point to the New Age introduced by Jesus Christ which renders the Old obsolete.

That this view is both an oversimplification and a falsification of the scriptural witness (both Old and New Testaments) becomes evident when one hears the prophetic announcement of God's requirements in the larger context of Israel's traditions. The Israelite story, which centers primarily in exodus and Sinai (traditions in Genesis are regarded as preparation, and the subsequent part of the Pentateuchal story as outcome) is fundamentally the amazing story of God's involvement in the life of his people. Yahweh "saw" the affliction of his people in Egypt, he "heard" their cry of distress under oppression, he "knew" their sufferings—and he decided to involve himself in their plight (Exod. 3:7–12). In the history of Israelite traditions, the theme of God's involvement was treated variously, depending on the situation in which the word of God was heard. Divine involvement could mean support in times of need (protection, vindication); in times of affluence, as in the period of the eighth century prophets, it could mean opposition (threat, judgment). Yet whether God's word was spoken "for" or "against" the people, or both, the fundamental theme of the story is that God cares—cares enough to get involved in the human story. The key text of Amos' preaching, following the NEB translation, was: "For you alone have I cared . . . therefore I will punish you . . ." (Amos 3:2). The other prophets, despite differences in theological accent, stood on the same conviction. Yahweh is the God who cares. He is not indifferent to Israel's way of life, but takes his people seriously. And he decided to be present with, and go with, Israel in her historical journey so that this people, *his* people, might be a paradigm to the world of what it means to be "known" or "cared for" by God.

THE PATHOS OF YAHWEH

At almost any place that we delve into the literature of the eighth century prophets we find that "passionate" language is ascribed to God. According to Amos, Yahweh "hates" Israel's religious ceremonies and "loathes" the pride of Jacob (Amos. 5:21; 6:8). Hosea uses the imagery of a husband disciplining a faithless wife or a father dealing with a prodigal son to portray Yahweh's relationship with his people (Hos. 2, 11). Isaiah's book opens with the Divine Parent's anguished disappointment over children who proved to be rebellious (Isa. 1:2–3). And running through the whole prophetic message are the themes of God's wrath and his compassion. Such passionate human language is indispensable in expressing God's involvement with his people, his entering into covenant relationship with them and addressing them as persons. The language of the prophets is in sharp contrast to the mystic's lapse into silence before the ineffable mystery of the Divine, or attempts to speak of God in impersonal terms such as Unmoved Mover, Ground of Being, Force of Growth, Principle of Order.

In his important book on *The Prophets,* to which we have referred from time to time, Abraham Heschel maintains that the "ground tone"—the deep diapason—of prophetic consciousness is God's *pathos* or "passion" (using the latter word in its older sense, as in "The Passion Story"). The God of the prophets, Heschel observes, "does not stand outside the range of human suffering and sorrow" in sovereign detachment or transcendent absoluteness; rather, "He is personally involved in, even stirred by, the conduct and fate of man." Heschel goes on to say: "He does not simply command and expect obedience; He is also moved and affected by what happens in the world, and reacts accordingly. Events and human actions arouse in Him joy or sorrow, pleasure or wrath. He is not conceived as judging the world in detachment. He reacts in an intimate and subjective manner, and thus determines the value of events."[14]

Those who have studied classical philosophy will realize that this prophetic view is novel and shocking. According to Plato and Aristotle, for instance, the supreme characteristic of deity is "apathy" (*apatheia*). God is Pure Being—beyond all human passion and struggle, untouched by concern or care, unaffected by the flux and transience of human history. In this perspective, God's transcendence means complete detachment from the world of human experience, cosmic indifference to the struggles and tragedies of human life. Many people, who have not read a word of the ancient philosophers, share this view in so far as they suppose that God is "up there" or "out there" somewhere in the cosmos but not "here," "with us," in human history. To them it would come as an intellectual shock to hear the proclamation that God, the Creator and Lord, is involved actively in the war against poverty and oppression, the struggle for human rights, or the agonizing and frustrating search for world order and peace.

As Blaise Pascal said in his *Meditations,* however, the God of the Bible is the God of Abraham, Isaac, and Jacob, not the God of the philosophers and the sages. "The Living God," to use a familiar biblical expression, is the One who is involved in living relationships, and hence is known relationally as the God *of* Abraham, or *of* Moses, or *of* the prophets. He is not apathetic, but passionately concerned, not transcendently aloof but personally and intimately related to the world. Divine pathos, to use Heschel's phraseology, is the expression of "a living care," "a dynamic relation between God and man."[15]

THE HOLY ONE IN YOUR MIDST

This "dynamic relation" is the subject of Hosea 11:1–11, the magnificent poem about Israel, Yahweh's prodigal son. One of the most moving passages in the Old Testament, the poem pulses with the heart of the prophetic message.[16] Here Yahweh's involvement with, and commitment to, his people is portrayed in imaginative language that is both anthropomorphic and anthropopathic: anthropomorphic in that God is "imaged" in human terms (Father in relation to son) and anthropopathic in that his anguish (pathos) is expressed with human feeling and passion.

The poem stands out as a separate literary pericope. It is abruptly introduced in verse 1 with a reference to the exodus, a theme that is unanticipated in the foregoing chapter 10; and it reaches a conclusion in verse 11 with the motif of "the new exodus" and the final messenger formula, "utterance of Yahweh." The next verse (v. 12 in English Bibles; 12:1 in the Hebrew Bible) seems to belong to the ensuing poem about Ephraim.

The poem itself deals with the problem of the refractory son—a problem that was important in Israelite society where family ties, family solidarity, and family inheritance were much more important than in modern societies that are governed by individualism and permissiveness. Indeed, there is a severe—and to modern sensitivities, a shocking—law in Deuteronomy 21:18–21 that prescribes what a father and mother were to do in the case of a reprobate son who violated the ancient commandment to honor his parents: he was to be handed over to the elders who held court in the city gate (cf. Amos 5:15, "justice in the gate") and, on the strength of valid parental complaint, was to receive the death penalty. It is not our purpose to evaluate this law; fortunately it has been superseded by more refined legal views. Rather, our concern is to understand how such a legal understanding is reinterpreted on a theological level, as the poet deals with the question: what shall be done in the case of Yahweh's "son," Israel, who has proven to be perpetually and incorrigibly obstinate?

The poem falls into two parts, each of which deals with a dimension of God's pathos.

A. The Pathos of Anger (11:1-7). In the first movement of the poem Yahweh speaks in the first person ("I"), but Israel is spoken *about* in the third person ("my son," "him," "them," and climactically in v. 7 "my people"). Yahweh's charge against his son is given in the manner of parents who might have spoken about their son, in his absence, at an inquiry held in the city gate. Yahweh testifies that he loved his son from infancy, that he called him out of Egypt and formed him as a people, that he taught him how to walk and lifted him in his arms, that he led him (them) "with bonds of love" and "lifted them like a little child to [his] cheek (vv. 1, 3, 4; see NEB). The entire history of Yahweh's dealings with his people was a history of divine care. BUT (this adversative runs heavily through the Parent's complaint) in spite of caring actions, they (Israel) became estranged and defiant, they did not know that he bound them to himself in love, they were bent on rebellion (vv. 2, 3, 4, 7). The "legal" way to handle such a refractory son was to issue the penalty of "death": Israel shall go back to Egypt, returning once again to slavery, this time under the yoke of Assyria (vv. 5-7).

B. The Pathos of Compassion (11:8-9, 11). In the second part of the poem Yahweh continues to speak in the first person, but the "son" is addressed directly ("you," "your"). The only exception to this dialogical style is verse 10, where Yahweh is referred to in the third person. But, in the judgment of many scholars, this verse, which lacks any clear metrical structure, may be a comment added later in prophetic tradition. In these verses we leave the situation of legal administration, where parents might have complained *about* their son in the city gate, and enter the realm of personal relationship in which Yahweh speaks *to* his son. Yahweh begins with a passionate outcry from his "heart," the depths of his being, in which he exclaims that his affection for his people prevents him from destroying them completely, as Admah and Zeboyim were obliterated in the holocaust that struck Sodom and Gomorrah (Gen. 19; Deut. 29:23). Despite their stubborn infidelity, he will not let them go; he will not destroy. The reason, introduced by the motive-particle *kî* ("for," "because"), is stated in the key sentence:

> For I am God and not man,
> the Holy One in your midst (Hos. 11:9b).

In the grace of God, the people will have a future. Hence, the poem ends with the motif of a new exodus: the people will return from foreign lands to their own homes (vv. 10–11).

According to this exquisite poem, Yahweh does not deal with his people on the basis of "law." Indeed, he is not bound by any "law" external to himself, whether the law of the first-born (cf. the choice of Jacob over Esau, Gen. 25) or any other social custom. As proclaimed in the Sinai tradition, he is free to be gracious unto whom he will be gracious, and to show mercy on whom he will show mercy (Exod. 33:19; cf. Rom. 9:15). There is something "irrational" in God's dealings with his people in that he goes beyond what they have a right to expect in terms of strict justice. It may be going too far to say that Yahweh waives the punishment completely and issues a "declaration of amnesty" (Wolff). Hosea knows that the people will suffer divine discipline in the context of the political realities of the time. Yahweh's judgment, however, will not be a sentence unto death, owing to compassion for his "son." As a psalmist said, meditating on Yahweh's grace (*hesed*), "He does not deal with us according to our sins, nor requite us according to our iniquities" (Ps. 103:10).

GOD'S STRANGE WORK

The prophets, too, agreed with the ancient confession, referred to in Psalm 103:8, that the God of Israel is "merciful and gracious, slow to anger, and abounding in steadfast love (*hesed*) and faithfulness" (Exod. 34:6). Yahweh's basic disposition toward his people is a steadfast faithfulness, a firm constancy based on his own gracious commitment. His wrath is "only for a moment," as a disciple of Isaiah said, but his loyalty lasts forever (Isa. 54:7–8).

Isaiah described Yahweh's wrath as his "strange deed," his "alien work" (Isa. 28:21). This language may be taken to imply a distinction between work that is "alien" and work that is "proper" to God's saving purpose. Here, again, the text must be understood in the context of the larger poem, Isaiah 28:7–22, which seems to be tacked on to earlier poetry about Ephraim, 28:1–4, 5–6.   According to the poem, Judah's inebriated leaders are no better than those of the northern kingdom which suffered destruction at the hand of Assyria.   To be sure, Judah has made a "covenant [treaty] with death," a reference to a diplomatic pact, probably with Egypt, that was intended to purchase security; but "the bed is too short," that is, the strategem will not work.   The God who uses justice as a plumbline (cf. Amos 7:7–9) will shatter the people's vaunted security by bringing a destructive storm upon them.   It is in this context that we read:

> For Yahweh will rise up as on Mount Perazim,
>> he will be wroth as in the valley of Gibeon,
> to do his deed—strange is his deed!
>> and to work his work—alien is his work! (Isa. 28:21)

Here the prophet recalls victories of the past: at Mount Perazim where David won a victory over the Philistines (2 Sam. 5:17–21), and at Gibeon where Joshua was victorious over a coalition of Amorites (Josh. 10:1–14).   In those times Yahweh had waged war *for* Israel; but, strangely, Yahweh is about to come as a Divine Warrior *against* his people.   In this context, Yahweh's wrathful action would appear "alien" or "strange" to those who expected that their well-laid diplomatic maneuvers—their "covenant with death"—would get them through the crisis, always in the confidence, of course, that their God would come to their rescue as he had in the past.   The God of Israel, however, is the God who does surprising things!   He performs shocking deeds in the midst of his own people!   At the same time, it is clear from this poem, as also from Hosea 11, that God's judgment ("wrath") is not antithetical to his saving purpose ("love").   His intention, according to Isaiah's prophecy, was to form in the crucible of suffering a new People, a new City—a chastened and purified remnant of grace that would represent a new beginning. According to a key verse in this poem, quoted several times in the New Testament, Yahweh was laying in Zion a foundation for the New Community, the New Jerusalem; and those who put their faith in God, rather than relying on political stratagems, would stand firm (cf. 7:9).

Look, I am laying a stone in Zion, a block of granite,
a precious corner-stone for a firm foundation;
he who has faith shall not waver

(Isa. 28:16, NEB).

There is, indeed, something "strange" about the prophetic language
concerning the "wrath" of God.   Normally we think of anger in psychological terms—as an emotional, perhaps uncontrollable, fit that
displays spite, recklessness, or violence.   Needless to say, such human
passion is unbecoming of the God who is faithful beyond all human
expectation and comprehension.   Israel's prophetic poets, however,
use passionate human language to lift our sights above the level of
human psychology to the theological level of God's involvement in
the life of his people.   His wrath, as Heschel has taught us to understand, is an aspect of his pathos—his passionate concern for his
people. The opposite of wrath is not love but indifference, apathy.
Only a God who is unconcerned and apathetic would be free from
the reaction of righteous indignation to human behavior.   In the
prophetic proclamation, God's wrath is inseparably related to his
concern for social justice, for there are some things that he will not
tolerate.   Indeed, for those who are victimized by various forms of
power (economic, imperial, legal, institutional), God's wrath may be
the basis for the hope that he will vindicate the oppressed by casting
down the "proud" and exalting those of low degree.

THE SHADOW OF GOD'S OUTSTRETCHED HAND

The question of how one deals with the scriptural theme of God's
wrath is of major concern in Christian proclamation.   Many Christians emphasize the affirmation, "God is love" (1 John 4:7,8)—one
dimension of the divine pathos that is exceedingly important in the
gospel of Jesus Christ (see Rom. 8:37–38).   Too often, however,
people selectively ignore passages in the New Testament that deal
with divine wrath, including Paul's announcement, found at the opening of his great theological treatise in the Epistle to the Romans, that
"the wrath of God is revealed from heaven" (Rom. 1:18; see also
such passages as Matt. 3:7; Luke 3:7; Eph. 2:3; 5:6; Col. 3:6;
1 Thess. 2:16; 5:9).   And, of course, much of the prophetic message
is ruled out of bounds from this standpoint.

Since both "wrath" and "love" are passionate terms, used by biblical poets to portray the depths of divine pathos, why is it that we are embarrassed, if not turned off completely, by biblical poems or parables that deal with God's wrath? In an illuminating chapter on "The Meaning and Mystery of Wrath," Heschel suggests that one source of our difficulty is the loss of poetic sensitivity to "spiritual grandeur." "Spiritual to us," he says, "means ethereal, calm, moderate, slight, imperceptible. We respond to beauty; grandeur is unbearable. We are moved by soft religiosity, and would like to think that God is lovely, tender, and familiar, as if faith were a source of comfort, but not readiness for martyrdom."[17] Others, for instance, Søren Kierkegaard, also have criticized sharply religious consciousness that is confined to the dimension of esthetics, never rising to the demanding level where the word of God is heard in the austerity and severity of holy love.

The eighth century prophets were keenly sensitive to "spiritual grandeur," for they were overwhelmed with the reality of the Holy One of Israel in their midst and of divine glory that filled the world. As poets they used vivid anthropomorphic and anthropopathic language to proclaim that Yahweh is personally related to the world, and personally involved with his people Israel. A striking illustration of this perception is the powerful poem in Isaiah 9:8—10:4, in which Isaiah, speaking after heavy disasters had befallen the northern kingdom (Ephraim), announced to Judeans in the South that Yahweh's hand was still outstretched. In five stanzas, if we adopt the suggestion to transpose a couple of verses from chapter 5 (vv. 24–25) to their appropriate context in chapter 9, the people are taken to task for:

A. their arrogant self-confidence (9:8–12)
B. the failure of leaders to lead rightly (9:13–17)
C. moral corruption that spreads like wildfire (9:18–21)
D. ignoring the claims of social justice (10:1–4)
E. neglecting religious teaching (5:24–25)

After each stanza comes the ominous refrain:

> For all this his anger is not turned away,
>> and his hand is stretched out still.

It is clear in this poem that the hand is stretched out in judgment—

as a threat to chastise a people that is stubbornly set in its ways and refuses to repent (cf. Amos 4:6–12). Yet when the poem is read in the larger context of the prophetic message it is clear that anger is not for anger's sake. Yahweh's wrath is the expression of his deep concern for his people, his passionate involvement with, and firm commitment to, them. In short, divine judgment is not the antithesis of divine love but is embraced within the mystery of "amazing grace" that will not let go of a people but wills redemption, restoration, and reconciliation. It was Hosea, above all, who sought to plumb the depth of Yahweh's amazing grace in dealing with Israel, especially in his poetic portrayals of the estranged wife (Hos. 2—3) and the prodigal son (Hos. 11). The shadow of Yahweh's outstretched hand brings the awareness of divine judgment, to be sure, but it is the judgment of the God whose anger is the dark side of love, whose compassion includes discipline, and who wills not to destroy but to lead to new life and maturity in covenant relationship. The sufferings of the present, as Francis Thompson found in his tumultuous experience, lie in the shadow of a hand stretched out to redeem.[18]

> All which I took from thee I did but take,
>   Not for thy harms,
> But just that thou might'st seek it in My arms.
>   All which thy child's mistake
> Fancies as lost, I have stored for thee at home:
>   Rise, clasp My hand, and come!
>
>   Halts by me that footfall:
>   Is my gloom, after all,
> Shade of His hand, outstretched caressingly?

CHAPTER EIGHT

WAITING FOR GOD

The eighth century prophets proclaimed their message in a situation which, on any realistic appraisal, provided no political ground for hope. Situated in the Mediterranean corridor between Mesopotamia and Egypt, through which powerful armies marched on their way to fulfill the dreams of world conquest, the Israelite people—both Ephraim and Judah—were eventually crushed between the upper and lower millstones of power politics. It is amazing that the literature of the Bible, which has influenced profoundly Western civilization and has given hope to millions of people, was composed in the setting of a small country and in a seemingly hopeless situation.

The prophets, as we have seen, were realists who announced to kings and people their ominous forebodings of catastrophe. Yet in spite of their pessimism about the immediate future, they were fundamentally theologians of hope. In the past, some scholars, demanding strict consistency, have argued that Amos and Hosea, Isaiah and Micah should be regarded as prophets of unmitigated doom. It is true that, when the prophetic books were finally edited for liturgical use, some optimistic passages were added to lighten and balance the somber tones of divine judgment. The appendix to the Book of Amos, for instance (Amos 9:11–15), with its themes of the restoration of the Davidic dynasty (the fallen "booth of David") and the coming of a glorious period of fertility, is out of keeping with the rest of his message and is generally regarded as a later addition. But even in this case, the expansion is based on an authentic note of Amos' preaching that we have considered previously: Yahweh desires his people to seek him and live (Amos 5:4–6, 14–15). Judgment and mercy, doom and restoration belong essentially to a full exposition of the prophetic message.

A major obstacle to understanding the prophetic message, at least until fairly recent times, has been a buoyant American optimism, oblivious to what has been called "the tragic dimension" of history. Confidence in our potentialities and faith in our destiny have made it difficult to cope with the intractable and frustrating realities of politics, evident in internal American turmoil (assassinations, violence, Watergate) and in external world affairs (Vietnam, the Middle East, East-West detente).   The prophets knew all too well "the tragic dimension"; yet, unlike Greek tragedians, they did not view people as being trapped hopelessly and helplessly in a no-exit situation, victims of an impersonal Fate that, sooner or later, would bring nemesis (retribution).   In a profound sense, the prophets were optimists. Their optimism, however, was based on Yahweh's faithfulness to his people—not on human possibility of reform or the political viability of the twin Israelite states, Ephraim and Judah.   Israel had been Yahweh's people before becoming a nation-state under Saul, David, and Solomon; and though Israel as a nation would inevitably go the way of all nations into defeat and destruction, Yahweh in his grace could and would raise up the people Israel in a new historical form (cf. Ezek. 37).   Accordingly, Paul could declare that in the mystery of God's wisdom and grace the Christian community, co-existing with the Jewish community, belongs to "the Israel of God" (Gal. 6:16; cf. Rom. 9—11).   Hence all people of faith are embraced within the promises of grace to Israel and may hear in the Old Testament "the gospel preached beforehand" (Gal. 3:8).

STRAINING TOWARD THE FUTURE

One of the key verbs for "hope" (*qwh*)—related to the word for a line that is pulled taught—suggests the idea of straining eagerly toward the future, tensely waiting through the night for God.   Thus we read in a great penitential psalm:

> I wait for Yahweh, my soul [being] waits,
>   and in his word I hope;
> my soul waits for Yahweh,
>   more than watchmen for the morning . . . (Ps. 130:5–6).

We have already encountered this motif in Hosea's proclamation, where he declared that a return to Yahweh would involve "practicing loyalty (*ḥesed*) and justice" and "waiting continually for your God" (Hos. 12:6). And, as we shall see, the motif of "waiting for Yahweh" is found in an important passage in the Book of Isaiah (8:16–22) where the prophet speaks to the circle of his disciples. In all of these cases, hope is not something different from faith, but is faith standing on tiptoe, as it were, and straining eagerly toward God's future when his word, spoken by the prophet, will be realized. Such faith, manifest in tensely awaiting Yahweh (see Isa. 40:31!), is a response to his faithfulness and loyalty (*ḥesed*).

We shall explore this theme by considering the way it is expressed in two kinds of poetic imagery: one rural and the other urban. In his portrayal of the future, Isaiah drew deeply upon the royal covenant theology tradition. He envisioned a New Jerusalem and a coming Anointed One ("messiah") whose rule would extend from the central metropolis throughout the earth. On the other hand, Hosea (like Jeremiah) was more influenced by Israel's ancient rural tradition that was rooted in an area removed from urban culture: the wilderness. Let us consider, first, how Hosea treats the theme of hope.

GRACE IN THE WILDERNESS

The wilderness, in which Israel wandered for "forty years," constitutes one of the central themes of Israel's Torah Story, along with "promises to the patriarchs," "exodus and Sinai," and "inheritance of the land." In the present form of the Pentateuchal story, the wilderness is portrayed as the time and place in which Israel murmured and complained, failing to see on every hand the benevolence and guidance of Yahweh. The wilderness, in this context, stood for rebellion. Hence remembering the stories of the wilderness could serve as a warning and a call to penitence (Ps. 95:8–11; cf. 1 Cor. 10:6–13).

In the proclamation of Hosea, however, the wilderness has a positive meaning. His summary of the Israelite story goes like this: a) It was in the wilderness that Yahweh "found Israel like grapes" on a vine (Hos. 9:10a), and he reacted with joy to his discovery. But b) "they came to Baal-peor" on the threshold of the promised land (cf. Num. 25:1–18) where they gave themselves to Baal, the god of fertility, "and became detestable like the thing they loved"

(9:10b). Hence c) if Israel is to have a future, she must return to the wilderness and recover the pristine relationship with God she had in the beginning. The wilderness, then, is the place of the eschatological new beginning. It is not surprising, in the light of this scriptural tradition, that messianic movements, like the Essenes of Qumran or John the Baptist's sect, were based in the wilderness. According to the Gospel of Mark, Jesus' ministry began in the wilderness (Mark 1:9–12), and to the wilderness he retreated from time to time (Mark 1:35, 45; cf. Luke 5:16).

Let us turn to the first part of the Book of Hosea (chaps. 1—3), and especially to a passage in 2:2–15 (+16–23) where the prophet picks up on the "Baal-peor" phase of the Israelite story summarized above. Making bold use of poetic license, he takes over the theme of the "sacred marriage" from Canaanite religion. This religion, very popular among the people as we learn from all the prophets, was based on another "story" or "myth." The story had to do with the sexual relation between the Baal god and his female consort, the mother goddess. The separation of god and goddess from each other resulted in the languishing of vegetation in the barren winter, with attendant rites of ritual mourning; and their sexual reunion made possible the revival of the powers of agricultural fertility, celebrated in the springtime with rejoicing and abandon. Farmers whose existence was tied to the rotation of the seasons believed that worshiping Yahweh in the manner of the Canaanite Baal was the way to adjust to the agricultural environment and to insure a thriving economy. Hosea sees the evidences of the economic boom, but he insists that the people have failed to understand the source of their life and welfare. Applying the myth of the sacred marriage to the Israelite story, he declares that Yahweh is the "husband" (Lord) and Israel is his "wife." The engagement between Yahweh and Israel originally occurred in the wilderness (Sinai), where Israel responded with the youthful love of a bride (cf. Jer. 2:2). But on entering the agricultural land, Israel was inflamed with "a spirit of harlotry" (Hos. 5:4) —a wild and reckless passion that drove her to abandon her true "husband" and to become a prostitute who received "wages" from passing strangers. The question is: How far can freedom go? What will Yahweh do with a people like this?

This is the question that prompts Yahweh, according to the

"kerygmatic unit" in Hosea 2:2–15 (Wolff, *Hosea,* pp. 31–33), to initiate a covenant lawsuit against his "wife," the "mother" of his children.   There were precedents for handling the case of an unfaithful wife in Israelite legal tradition (cf. Deut. 22:13–21), though it is fortunate that such cases, which presuppose a strictly patriarchal society, have been superseded by subsequent judicial developments (certainly in our own time).   The point of the "legal controversy," however, is not to absolutize a particular understanding of masculine-feminine relations but to lift the whole discussion up to a metaphorical level, that is, the relation between Yahweh, Israel's "first husband" (2:7b) and Israel, his "wife" (2:2a).   The poem falls into two parts.

A. *Argument of the case* (2:2–5).   The Hebrew verbs are in the plural ("contend with, plead a case against") because the children (Israelites) are brought into court to confirm the testimony against Mother Israel.   The burden of the accusation is that Israel, on entering the agricultural land, betrayed her Husband who had lavished his affection on her; for she turned to other "lovers," supposing that economic blessings were the "wages" given for prostitution.

B. *Court verdict* (2:6–15).   The punishment, already indicated as a possibility in the first part ("lest I . . . ," vv. 3–4), is announced explicitly by Yahweh who is plaintiff, judge, and executor of the judgment.   Notice that this part of the poem falls into three strophes, each punctuated by the consequential word, "therefore."

Therefore, given the wife's harlotrous conduct, Yahweh will shut off the paths that lead to her lovers in the hope that she will "return" to the fulfilling first relationship (vv. 6–8).

Therefore Yahweh will take back his own gifts, which his wife falsely understood as payment from her paramours, and will terminate "the feast days of the Baals" during which she "forgot" her true husband (vv. 9–13).

Therefore. . . . (vv. 14–15).

THE GATEWAY OF HOPE

It is with the climactic "therefore" that we are primarily concerned here.   The court scene breaks up with the announcement of something startlingly new, something that goes beyond legal precedent or requirement: Yahweh proposes to "allure" his wife (the verb is also used of seducing a woman, Exod. 22:15!)—to lead her into the wilderness and there make love to her (literally, "speak to her heart"). "From there," as the Hebrew reads, "he will give her her vineyards (that is, the produce of a fertile soil) and the Valley of Achor as a door of hope." In that wilderness setting, away from the enticements of city culture, she will respond spontaneously "as in the days of her youth, as in the time when she came out of the land of Egypt."

The Valley of Achor apparently is the *Buqē'a*, a valley situated in the desolate Judean desert west of the Dead Sea, near the present orthodox monastery of Mar Saba. Those who have ventured into this barren region realize that the valley is just above the ancient monastery of Qumran, at a point on the West Bank where the land ascends to the fertile country with its vineyards. The reference to Achor is surprising in this context, however, for according to the "conquest tradition" of the Book of Joshua, Israel penetrated the West Bank farther north, in the region of Ai and Bethel (Josh. 7—8). It may be that Hosea intends to draw a typological contrast between the old exodus and the new. After the original exodus, Israel entered the promised land through a gateway that led to Achor, a place of flagrant sin (Josh. 7:20-26). The new exodus of salvation, however, will lead to a different area—to the wilderness further south and "from there" Israel will receive her vineyards as a token of a new relationship, a new covenant with God.

The poetic imagery, however, cannot be reduced to geography. The wilderness symbolizes a historical situation in which Israel is stripped of illusory securities and in which false loyalties are shown to be hollow. The prophets understood that people are moulded by their heart's desire: that those who "pursue empty phantoms, themselves become empty" (Jer. 2:5, NEB); and that those who love what is loathsome, themselves become abhorrent (Hos. 9:10b). Furthermore, as Luther observed, "Whatever then thy heart clings to and relies upon, that is properly thy God." Hence a crisis of faith may be an identity crisis when pressing questions are raised: "What, or who, is your god?" "Is your God great enough to save you?" For Hosea, the "wilderness" was a place where these questions would find an answer—where Israel would rediscover who her God is and thus her identity as a people. There she would "respond as in the days of her youth" to the grace that called her into being and gave her a future. "The people who survived the sword, found grace in the wilderness" (Jer. 31:2). In the retrospect of faith, then, God's judgment would prove to be his salvation.

Let us not ignore the "tragic dimension" of the biblical witness. The path into the future is along a *via dolorosa*, a pathway of suffering for both God and his people. Hosea understands, as do other prophets, that suffering is a catharsis, a purgation for a people who must reap the consequences of their false commitments. He also knows, perhaps more profoundly than other eighth century prophets, that Yahweh himself suffers in his gracious commitment to his people. Wolff comments on the final "therefore" of the covenant lawsuit in words that suggest this divine pathos: "God suffers under Israel's deceitful love affair . . . his love unrequited, he laments that he is forgotten. . . . Because God suffers in his love for Israel, he *therefore* [italics added] woos her once again."[19]   It is in the "wilderness" of suffering, the "wasteland" of disappointed love, that the Valley of Achor may become "the gateway of hope."

The tones struck by Hosea reverberate in later prophetic tradition. The proclamation of so-called Second Isaiah (Isa. 40—55) opens with a poem of consolation which echoes Hosea's motif that Yahweh wants to "speak to the heart" of the people (Isa. 40:1; cf. Hos. 2:14–15), that is, to take the initiative in renewing the relationship. Furthermore, this prophet proclaims the good news that in the "wilderness" the people of God will find a new road that leads into the future.

> In the wilderness, prepare the way of Yahweh;
> Make straight in the desert a highway for our God!
> (Isa. 40:3)

In the New Testament the prophetic proclamation of the new beginning in the wilderness is transposed into a new key (see Mark 1:3).

WHEN GOD HIDES HIS FACE

We turn, now, to another poetic way of imagining the future, one that is associated primarily with the City. The passage that will engage our attention is the well-known portrayal of the future Anointed One, the "messianic" king (Isa. 9:1–7). It is important, however, to understand this literary unit not only in its original life situation but in its present literary context. The poem stands at the climax of a separate booklet (Isa. 6:1—9:7) that has been inserted into the heart of a sequence of woes and refrains about Yahweh's outstretched hand: 5:8–30 on the one side, and 9:8—10:19 on the other. The booklet is a prose account interspersed with poetry and is essentially autobiographical in character, as evidenced by the repeated use of the first personal pronoun "I," "me," "my." It begins with the account of Isaiah's call (chap. 6) and concentrates especially on the crisis of the Syro-Ephraimitic War (7:1–17). [See chronological chart, p. 4.]

The materials in chapter 8 reflect this great political and spiritual crisis which presented the prophet with his greatest problem: the people's insensitivity to the call for faith, a matter introduced at the very beginning of the booklet (Isa. 6:9–13). King Ahaz himself, it will be recalled, rejected the prophet's counsel and cast himself on the mercy of Tiglath-pileser (2 Kings 16: 5–9). Out of this situation came the ominous name, Maher-shalal-hash-baz ("The spoil speeds, the prey hastens"), given one of Isaiah's sons to signify that the threat of the Syro-Ephraimitic coalition would be ended by Assyrian invasion (8:1–4).

We then find a little poem dealing with a theme that we have considered previously: the people who rejected the gently flowing waters of Shiloah (the life-giving springs of faith in God) and placed their confidence in Assyrian rule will be overwhelmed with a destructive flood from the Euphrates (8:5–10). Twice in this poem the poet refers to the sign-child Immanuel (vv. 8, 10), the intention being to show that the devastating political catastrophe does not mean that Assyria is in control. The nations are warned that their plans will be foiled, their word will not stand, "for God is with us."

What, then, is to be "the role of the prophet among people who will not hear"?—to cite a caption in the NEB annotations to this chapter. The answer to this question is given in the autobiographical prose passage in 8:11–15, 16–22. The first part (8:11–15) opens with an oracle to the prophet in which Yahweh spoke "with his strong hand upon me," warning him "not to walk in the way of this people."

Yahweh's word to him is also addressed to others (as evidenced by the plural forms in Hebrew)—to the remnant whose faith gives them a different perspective and a higher loyalty. Specifically, the oracle warns against confidence in any political alliance:

> Call not alliance what this people calls alliance,
>   and fear not, nor stand in awe of what they fear.
> But with Yahweh of hosts make your alliance—
>   let him be your fear and your awe (Isa. 8:12–13, NAB).

Here again we encounter the theme of the humble walk with God.

It is in the second part of this autobiographical testimony that we find the theme of hope, or "waiting for Yahweh" (8:16–18, 19–22). Since neither king nor people would listen, the prophet decided to go into seclusion for a while and to bind up and seal his teaching among his disciples.

> For I will trust in Yahweh,
>   who is hiding his face from the house of Jacob;
>   yes, I will wait for him (Isa. 8:17, NAB).

In this passage several things deserve attention. First, the time is understood as one when Yahweh "hides his face," that is, his presence. Worshipers then, as still today, went to the temple to be in God's presence, or to use the language of a psalmist, to "seek Yahweh's face" (Ps. 27:7–8). But when the prophetic word, with its radical call to faith, is no longer heard in the community, the time becomes one of God's silence or, as Amos put it, a time of "famine of hearing the words of Yahweh" (Amos 8:11–12). When the people refuse to listen, the prophetic word is treasured in the small community of disciples, a kind of "church within the church," which lives by faith and waits for the time when the prophetic scroll will be unsealed and a future generation will understand.

Second, the oral word of the prophet is not only written down as literature and sealed for the future, but the message is "embodied" in the prophet's family. "Behold, I and the children whom Yahweh has given me are signs and portents in Israel from Yahweh of hosts who dwells on Mount Zion" (8:18). The naming of children is one way that the prophet attempted to give concreteness and actuality to Yahweh's word (cf. Hos. 1). Commentators have noted that the names of the sons are, in a profound sense, expositions of the meaning of their father's name Isaiah, which in Hebrew means "Yahweh is salvation." The name of the oldest child, Shear-yashub ("A remnant shall return"), embodies the theme that a remnant will be purified in the fires of catastrophe and return to God. The name of the younger child, Maher-shalal-hash-baz, is heavy with the theme of divine judgment. Taken together, these names signify the central prophetic proclamation that God will lead his people through judgment toward deliverance. Indeed, the sign-name of Immanuel (7:15), alluded to twice in chapter 8 (vv. 8, 10), was also pregnant with the meaning of divine judgment and mercy and pointed beyond the immediate crisis of the Syro-Ephraimitic War to the new age, the kingdom of God, that would lie beyond tragedy.

Finally, the prophet's appeal to the future time when the face of God will no longer be hidden, is made in the name of "Yahweh of hosts who dwells on Mount Zion" (8:18b). Here again we find the basic theological conviction of Isaiah: that Yahweh, the Lord of all heavenly and earthly powers (hosts), has chosen to bind himself in grace to the Davidic king and has selected the sanctuary on Mount Zion as the place of his sacramental presence. The verb translated "dwell" (*šākan*) seems to recall the ancient motif of Yahweh "tabernacling" or "tenting" in the midst of his people, as in the Tent of Meeting (Exod. 33:7–11). Yahweh does not "live" in the temple, as though it were his home; rather, he "comes down" on occasion to be present with his worshiping people, to tabernacle or "tent" in their midst (cf. John 1:14, "he tented among us"). It is not surprising, then, that the Book of Isaiah includes the exquisite poem, found in Isaiah 2:2–4 (also Mic. 4:1–4), which portrays the consummation of history as a time when all peoples will make a pilgrimage to Zion, the center of the earth and the place of Yahweh's presence, from which his word goes forth. The Holy One is free to disclose his majesty anywhere in the world and in any way that he chooses; but if people would have access to him, they must come to the rendezvous that he has designated. As the Old Testament theologian, Walther Eichrodt, observes: "Not everywhere in the world can one at random seek him, not in abstract generalities are his revelations given; but here, at a particular place, in the situation of one of the peoples of the ancient Near East that was concretely determined by historical factors, the God who holds the whole world in his hands wills to reveal himself, to be known, and to be apprehended."[20] In the Fourth Gospel, the symbolism of the centrality of the temple is reinterpreted to refer to Jesus' own person (John 2:19), as the Living Center of the New Community.

WAITING FOR THE DAWN

Thus the various vignettes in Isaiah 8 present a picture of darkness, illumined only by the prophetic word that strains toward God's future and that is treasured in a small waiting community of disciples. Over the chapter as a whole falls the heavy shadow of Assyrian imperial might and specifically the crisis of the Syro-Ephraimitic War. People and king, anxious about their uncertain future, attempted to purchase security by whatever human means available. Not only did this lead to playing the usual game of power politics, but many people, lacking the power to make the political decisions that affected their destiny, turned to various forms of superstition. They consulted spiritual mediums and necromancers (Isa. 8:19–20) in the hope of peering beyond the veil of the future, just as people try to cope with the insecurities of the atomic age by resorting to astrology, spiritualism, and various occult arts. Isaiah's response is that there is no future in this sort of thing; it is another evidence that the people refuse to walk humbly with their God. What the mediums and clairvoyants have to say "is futile" (NEB); or, as RSV translates, "Surely for this word which they speak there is no dawn." Only those who cast themselves in faith upon God's prophetic word of judgment and mercy, waiting expectantly for its realization, look forward to the dawn of God's future.

It is in this context that we find the magnificent poem in Isaiah 9:2–7 about the wonder-child who will sit on the throne of Jerusalem and reign as God's representative on earth. The connection of the poem with the autobiographical material dealing with the Syro-Ephraimitic War (7:1—8:15) is evident in several ways. First, the initial note, "the people who walked in darkness have seen a great light," ties in with the preceding theme of darkness that falls over those who reject the word of the prophet and turn, instead, to spiritual mediums and fortune-tellers who "chirp and mutter" (8:21–22).

Furthermore, the transitional sentence in 9:1 places the poem in the context of the political crisis reflected in chapters 7 and 8 by referring specifically to the invasion of the Assyrian king, Tiglath-pileser III, into northern Israel in 733–732 B.C. (2 Kings 15:29) along "the way of the sea," that is, the road leading from Damascus to the Mediterranean. Finally, in this editorial context the portrayal of the wonder-child is intentionally related to the sign of the Immanuel child mentioned in 7:14–17 and the Immanuel overtones that reverberate in the following chapter (8:8, 10).

Although the poem was placed in this literary context by Isaiah or, more likely, his prophetic disciples, the poem undoubtedly was composed as a separate piece for a particular setting in life. Let us notice the structure and movement of the poem, following the author's annotated translation.

A. 9:2–3. The poem begins with a portrayal of those who dwell in "the shadow of death" (cf. Ps. 23:4), that is, dismal darkness.

> The people who walk in darkness have seen a great light;
>> upon those who dwell in the land of death's shadow light has dawned.

This "light," however, is perceptible to those whose faith is in God, as indicated by the "thou" form of thanksgiving.

> You have increased their joy,
>> you have magnified their gladness.

The people's joy is described in terms of two familiar experiences: celebration at the ingathering of the harvest and at the end of war.

> They are glad before you as at harvest gladness,
>> and they rejoice as when the spoil of war is divided.

B. 9:4–6b. The poet now turns to the specific reasons for the people's rejoicing. Three motives are given, each introduced by the motive-word "for" (*kî*).

> For his burdensome yoke,
>> the collar over his shoulders,
>> the goad for driving him,
>> you shatter as on the Day of Midian.

For every warrior's shoe with heavy heel,
    every uniform soaked with blood,
    will be for burning, fuel for fire.

For a child is born for us,
    a son is granted to us,
    and the dominion will rest on his shoulders.

Notice how these *kî*-verses ascend to a great climax! The first announcement refers to the past—to the victory over Midian achieved
by God's power with slender human resources (Judges 6—8). In
this manner, as Israel's history shows, God has shattered again and
again the people's yoke of slavery and has granted freedom. The
second announcement is futuristic: the time is coming when the
rules of the game of politics will be changed and people will study
war no more (cf. Isa. 2:4). The third announcement employs verbs
which herald a glorious event, an event that is an actuality in the
sense that it is firmly fixed in the purpose of God, though not yet
fully realized. The splendor of the new age that God intends to
inaugurate is signified by the birth of a wonder-child who will ascend
the throne and take the reins of government.

   C. 9:6c–7. The final part of the poem, if our outline is correct,
provides an exalted portrayal of the attributes of the coming king
and the character of his rule.

His name will be called:
    Wonderful counsellor,
    Divine Hero,
    Father perpetually,
    Prince of peace.

Great will be the dominion, and no end to peace,
    upon the throne of David, and over his kingdom,
    to establish it and to support it
    with justice and righteousness
    from now unto endless time.

The poem ends with a coda which announces that this wonderful
new age will come not through human striving, but through the
"zeal" or energetic determination of God's will.

The fervency of Yahweh of hosts will accomplish this!
(Isa. 9:7d).

THE NEW AGE

Isaiah's poem strikes a response deep in the hearts of people in every age who, weary with wars and bloodshed, long for a new administration that will inaugurate a peaceful regime in which there will be welfare within the community and freedom from external threat. These human sentiments are customarily expressed on great festival occasions, such as a turning point in the year (Christmas, New Year's) or the inauguration of a new administration. It is possible that Isaiah's poem, which now functions in a specific *literary* context, once was related to a concrete *life* situation, perhaps the celebration of the birth of a crown prince or the coronation of a king. Such court poetry was well-known in the ancient world, for instance in Egypt, where a coronation ceremony included the granting of a "protocol" to the new king in which the deity offered the scepter of dominion, the bestowal of various elevated titles befitting the new ruler, and the assurance of peaceful and beneficial rule. Psalms 2 and 110 seem to presuppose such a coronation ceremony in Israel. On such occasions, as we can well understand, the most extravagant court language was used in praising the new ruler, even language that accorded him divine honor! Remember that Isaiah stood firmly within the royal covenant theology which emphasized Yahweh's promises of grace to David and the centrality of Zion. He had reminded King Ahaz that a plot to overthrow the Davidic king would fail, and he offered the Immanuel sign as an assurance of Yahweh's commitment to the house (dynasty) of David. So, Isaiah may have been a kind of poet laureate who composed his poem to honor the birth of a new heir to the Davidic throne, conferring on him the dominion assured to a king who rules as the representative of Yahweh and extolling him with four exalted throne names (9:6). As we noticed earlier, Isaiah's Immanuel sign referred to the birth of a child in the very near future, possibly in the Davidic household. The child would live through trying experiences and eventually ascend the throne of Judah where, in contrast to faithless King Ahaz, he would rule righteously. Some have suggested that the "young woman" referred to in Isaiah 7:14 was the wife of Ahaz and that her son, the Immanuel child, was to be the future king, Hezekiah.

It is difficult, however, to turn the poetry of prophecy into the prose of history. Even though Isaiah's Immanuel prophecy was related concretely to the crisis of the Syro-Ephraimitic War, there is an aura of mystery about the Immanuel sign and about the poetic portrayal of the wonder-child in Isaiah 9:1–9 (which, in the present literary context, is editorially connected with Immanuel). Apparently the poet drew upon ancient mythical tradition concerning the renewal of the primeval state of peace, undisturbed by historical violence and competition, and the coming of a King who would be endowed with such supernatural gifts that his administration would combine perfectly power and goodness, authority and wisdom. But has such an administration ever occurred? Who ever heard of turning to a defenseless child as a symbol of power? or of an administration that would scrap the accoutrements of war? or of a king who is worthy of the titles that are here bestowed ("Wonderful counsellor . . . Prince of peace")? The poetic portrayal hardly corresponds to any political regime of the Davidic monarchy or, for that matter, to any administration known in history up to the present time. The late, distinguished Old Testament theologian, Gerhard von Rad, observed that portrayals like this are suffused with such a *doxa* ("glory") that the people could appropriately ask with mingled doubt and hope, as did John the Baptist (Matt. 11:3): "Are you he who is to come, or shall we look for another?"[21]

Thus Isaiah's poetry, though addressed to his immediate situation, reverberates with meanings that transcend the political realities of his time. In his vision, the kingdom of God surpasses the ordinary political sphere in which people, then as now, placed their confidence in armies, weapons, fortifications, and treaties, hoping to gain thereby some temporary and provisional security against the uncertainties of the future. But his prophetic word was too difficult for an arrogant people, stubbornly committed to their way of life, to hear. Therefore, he sealed his teaching among his disciples in written form so that distant generations, perhaps our own, might read and understand under new circumstances. "I will wait for Yahweh, who is hiding his face from the house of Jacob, and I will hope in him" (Isa. 8:17).

The seal on Isaiah's teaching was first broken by one of his later disciples (Second Isaiah), also a poet, who lived during the period of the Babylonian Exile. At that time the people again found it hard to believe in God in face of the hard facts of suffering: the destruction of a nation, the uprooting of a people, the dashing of human hopes. The prophet proclaimed, however, that Yahweh's word spoken by his prophets stands forever—in perpetuity (Isa. 40:8)— in contrast to political promises based on transient human achievements and finite human wisdom. God is faithful, beyond all human infidelity and surpassing all human wisdom; hence faith is manifest in waiting for Yahweh with tense expectation of the "new thing" (Isa. 43:18-19) that he will do.

> They who wait for Yahweh shall renew their strength,
>   they shall mount up with wings like eagles,
> they shall run and not be weary,
>   they shall walk and not faint
>   (Isa. 40:31; cf. Isa. 8:17).

The seal on Isaiah's teaching was also broken in the proclamation of the New Testament. In Christian perspective, Jesus of Nazareth is the Immanuel sign who confirms and actualizes the prophetic word that calls to faith, the very word spoken by Isaiah to King Ahaz in a time of political insecurity and spoken to distant generations, including our own. Faith still strains toward the future, waiting in hope for the time when the tensions of life will be resolved and the evils of history will be overcome, when God's kingdom will be secured "with justice and with righteousness from this time forth and for evermore" (Isa. 9:7c).[22]

NOTES

1. *Luther's Works,* ed. Helmut T. Lehmann (Philadelphia: Fortress, 1960), vol. 35, *Word and Sacrament I,* ed. E. Theodore Bachmann, p. 274.
2. Karl Jaspers, "The Axial Age of Human History," *Identity and Anxiety: Survival of the Person in Mass Society,* ed. Maurice R. Stein, Arthur J. Vidlich, and David Manning White (Glencoe, Ill.: Free Press, 1960), pp. 597–605.
3. Johannes Lindblom, *Prophecy in Ancient Israel* (Philadelphia: Fortress, 1962), p. 311.
4. For a retelling of the story in modern newspaper style, see *Chronicles: News of the Past,* vol. 1 (Jerusalem, Israel: The Reubeni Foundation, 1968), Issues 22, 23, 24, American distributor: C. Zanziper, N.Y.
5. Abraham J. Heschel, *The Prophets* (New York: Harper and Row, 1965), p. 22.
6. Edmund Jacob, *Theology of the Old Testament,* trans. A. W. Heathcote and P. J. Allcock (New York: Harper and Row, 1958), p. 290. In this connection I would like to draw attention especially to the essay by Hans Walter Wolff, "Die eigentliche Botschaft der klassichen Propheten" ("The Central Message of the Classical Prophets"), published in a Festschrift for Walther Zimmerli, *Beiträge zur alttestamentlichen Theologie* (Göttingen: Vandenhoeck and Ruprecht, 1977), pp. 547–557. Wolff disagrees with Martin Buber who says that the basic note of prophetic preaching is a call to repentance and insists, rather, that prophetic preaching began with the announcement of God's coming to judge his people.
7. See Wilhelm Vischer's sermon, "Perhaps the Lord will be Gracious," *Interpretation,* 13 (1959): 286–295.
8. The quotation is from a study by J. M. Berridge, "Zur Intention der Botschaft des Amos' ("On the Intention of the Message of Amos"), *Theologische Zeitschrift,* 32 (1976), pp. 321–340, who provides an illuminating stylistic study of the structure of Amos 5.
9. Heschel, *The Prophets,* p. 187.

10. Gerhard von Rad, *Old Testament Theology*, trans. D. M. G. Stalker, vol. 2 (New York: Harper and Row, 1965), p. 198.
11. Hans Walter Wolff, *Hosea*, ed. Paul D. Hanson, trans. Gary Stansell, Hermeneia Series (Philadelphia: Fortress, 1974), p. 214.
12. Wolff, *Hosea*, p. 67.
13. Heschel, *The Prophets*, p .139.
14. Heschel, *The Prophets*, pp. 223–224; all of chapters 12–15 are important in this connection. The theme of divine pathos is emphasized by Jürgen Moltmann, *The Crucified God*, trans. R. A. Wilson and John Bowden (New York: Harper and Row, 1974), pp. 270–274.
15. Heschel, *The Prophets*, p. 224.
16. In his article on "Prophets, Prophetism," B. Davie Napier maintains that Hosea 11 contains the central themes of classical prophecy: word and symbol, election and covenant, rebellion, judgment, compassion, and redemption. See *The Interpreter's Dictionary of the Bible* (Nashville: Abingdon, 1962), pp. 869–919, especially 910–919.
17. Heschel, *The Prophets*, p. 296.
18. Francis Thompson, "The Hound of Heaven," *Complete Poems of Francis Thompson*, The Modern Library (New York: Random House, n.d.).
19. Wolff, *Hosea*, p. 44.
20. Walther Eichrodt, *Der Heilige in Israel: Jesaja 1–12 (The Holy One in Israel: Isaiah 1–12)*, (Stuttgart: Calwer Verlag, 1960) p. 97.
21. Gerhard von Rad, *Old Testament Theology*, vol. 1, pp. 323–324.
22. At the conclusion of this work I would like to thank several persons for their help: my wife, Joyce, who has shared this project with me and to whom the book itself is dedicated; my daughter, Carol Hanawalt, who has given careful editorial assistance; and my two graduate students, Larry L. Bethune and Bennie C. Ollenburger, who have checked the final manuscript.

SELECTED BIBLIOGRAPHY

General works on prophecy:

ANDERSON, BERNHARD W. *Understanding the Old Testament.* 3d ed. Englewood Cliffs, N.J.: Prentice-Hall, 1975, chapters 8—10.

HESCHEL, ABRAHAM J. *The Prophets.* New York: Harper & Row, 1963.

LINDBLOM, JOHANNES. *Prophecy in Ancient Israel.* Philadelphia: Fortress, 1962.

NAPIER, B. DAVIE. "Prophet, Prophetism." *The Interpreter's Dictionary of the Bible.* Nashville: Abingdon, 1962.

RAD, GERHARD VON. *The Message of the Prophets.* Translated by D. M. G. Stalker. London: SCM, 1968. Based on his discussion in *Old Testament Theology,* vol. 2. New York: Harper & Row, 1965.

SCOTT, R. B. Y. *The Relevance of the Prophets.* Rev. ed. New York: Macmillan, 1968.

VAWTER, BRUCE. *The Conscience of Israel.* New York: Sheed & Ward, 1961.

Commentaries on individual eighth century prophets:

MAYS, JAMES L. *Amos.* Old Testament Library. Philadelphia: Westminster, 1969.

WARD, JAMES M. *Amos and Isaiah: Prophets of the Word of God.* Nashville: Abingdon, 1969.

WOLFF, HANS WALTER. *Joel and Amos.* Hermeneia Series. Edited by S. Dean McBride, Jr. Philadelphia: Fortress, 1977.

BRUEGGEMANN, WALTER. *Tradition for Crisis: A Study in Hosea.* Richmond: John Knox, 1968.

MAYS, JAMES L. *Hosea.* Old Testament Library. Philadelphia: Westminster, 1969.

WARD, JAMES M. *Hosea: A Theological Commentary.* New York: Harper & Row, 1966.

WOLFF, HANS WALTER. *Hosea.* Hermeneia Series. Edited by Paul Hanson. Philadelphia: Fortress, 1974.

KAISER, OTTO. *Isaiah 1–12. Isaiah 13–39.* Translated by R. A. Wilson. Old Testament Library. Philadelphia: Westminster, 1972, 1974.

KISSANE, EDWARD J. *The Book of Isaiah,* 2 vols. rev. ed. Dublin: Browne & Nolan, 1960.

VRIEZEN, THEODORUS C. "Essentials of the Theology of Isaiah." *Israel's Prophetic Heritage.* Edited by B. W. Anderson and Walter Harrelson. New York: Harper & Row, 1962.

MAYS, JAMES L. *Micah.* Old Testament Library. Philadelphia: Westminster, 1976.

INDEX OF
BIBLICAL PASSAGES

References to passages from the Pericope Index on page xvi
are in boldface type.